SHAUN SPIERS

C000224973

HOW TO BUILD HOUSES *AND* SAVE THE COUNTRYSIDE

POLICY PRESS SHORTS INSIGHTS

First published in Great Britain in 2018 by

Policy Press
University of Bristol
1-9 Old Park Hill
Bristol
BS2 8BB
UK
t: +44 (0)117 954 5940
pp-info@bristol.ac.uk
www.policypress.co.uk

North America office:
Policy Press
c/o The University of Chicago Press
1427 East 60th Street
Chicago, IL 60637, USA
t: +1 773 702 7700
f: +1 773 702 9756
sales@press.uchicago.edu
www.press.uchicago.edu

British Library Cataloguing in Publication Data
A catalogue record for this book is available from the British Library.

Library of Congress Cataloging-in-Publication Data
A catalog record for this book has been requested.

ISBN 978-1-4473-3999-1 (paperback)
ISBN 978-1-4473-4663-0 (ePub)
ISBN 978-1-4473-4664-7 (Mobi)
ISBN 978-1-4473-4665-4 (ePDF)

Cover design by Policy Press
Front cover: image kindly supplied by Getty
Printed and bound in Great Britain by CMP, Poole
Policy Press uses environmentally responsible print partners

For Louise, Esther and Nye, who put up with me writing this, and for Abigail, who made helpful suggestions. Also for the Campaign to Protect Rural England's heroic volunteers and staff, standing up for the countryside.

Contents

List of figures

About the author

Shaun Spiers is executive director of the environmental think tank Green Alliance. He chairs the board of Greener UK, a coalition of 13 leading environmental groups campaigning to ensure the greenest possible Brexit, and is a trustee of Sustain, the alliance for better food and farming.

From 2004 to 2017, Shaun was chief executive of the Campaign to Protect Rural England (CPRE), a national charity that campaigns for a beautiful and living countryside. Founded in 1926, CPRE helped shape the modern planning system. It has a strong record both of protecting the countryside and promoting urban regeneration. CPRE's 43 county branches protect green spaces and help shape local plans. CPRE has over 2,000 member parish councils, many of which are involved in developing neighbourhood plans.

Before joining CPRE, Shaun ran ABCUL, the credit union trade association. From 1994 to 1999, he was the Labour and Co-operative MEP for South-East London.

Acknowledgements

I undertook to write this book when I was working for CPRE. Shortly afterwards, I took a new job with Green Alliance. CPRE's Chair, Su Sayer, and her fellow trustees generously gave me paid leave during my notice period to work on the book. Green Alliance's Chair, Fiona Reynolds, and my new colleagues were patient with me as I worked on this book when I should have been fully focused on my new role. I am grateful to both CPRE and Green Alliance. Neither organisation is in any way responsible for the views expressed here.

Martin Crookston gave me the idea for the book: he is not responsible for its contents, but I have drawn on some of his ideas. Trinley Walker and Camilla Zerr at CPRE commented on drafts, chased references and helped in many other ways. A number of CPRE members participated in three focus groups in Kent, Leicestershire and Oxfordshire, facilitated by Trinley. Oliver Hilliam and Paul Miner helped check facts and references. Matthew Williams gave me information on the Wymondham neighbourhood plan. Sue Chalkley, Martin Crookston, Fiona Howie, Su Sayer, Jane Seymour, Abigail Adams-Spiers and Matt Thomson generously commented on draft chapters. I am extremely grateful to everyone for their help and advice.

I have, of course, learnt from countless people, both in CPRE and other, sometimes opposing, organisations. Planning is fascinating (really, it is) and full of people (mostly) trying to do the right thing. Urbed is one of the most imaginative planning outfits, and I am grateful to David Rudlin and Nicholas Falk for letting me quote from the unpublished CPRE/Urbed joint statement, which they developed with Martin Crookston and Neil Sinden.

Many thanks to Jamie Askew, Emily Watt, Ruth Wallace, Susannah Emery and the team at Policy Press for their support.

My family came to hate 'the bloomin' book', but they gave me space to write it. My biggest thanks are to them.

Foreword

To many people, Shelter and the Campaign to Protect Rural England must seem like unlikely bedfellows. Shelter is typically associated with strident demands for more new homes to help hard-pressed city-dwellers facing homelessness. CPRE attracts almost the opposite caricature: that of the genteel campaign for well-off NIMBYs determined to preserve their corner of rural affluence. When I first met Shaun Spiers, not long after he'd taken the helm at CPRE, I asked him what had drawn him to the role, and was genuinely taken aback when he said it was because he'd always been an environmentalist. From my London-centric, housing obsessive viewpoint I had never thought of CPRE as an environmental campaign.

It's not hard to see where these stereotypes come from. Shelter is indeed preoccupied with the desperate lack of homes that underpins our mounting homelessness crisis. And CPRE members have indeed fought many a battle against new homes being built, up and down the country. Campaigning is hard, and often thankless work. The experience of fighting powerful vested interests, remote governments, stifling bureaucracies and sheer public indifference can be draining. It encourages campaigners to take clearer, simpler positions that might just get some attention. But taking strong positions tends to mean saying no to things, and defining the other side as the enemy. The longer campaigns go on, the deeper those divisions grow – feeding negative stereotypes and encouraging further retrenchment on both sides.

I've met liberal economists who think the abolition of all planning controls would deliver utopian outcomes for everyone. And I've encountered Green Belt campaigners who insist that a derelict petrol station on a main road in inner London must not be redeveloped for social housing, because it happened to be classified as Green Belt. It's easy to deride this as narrow intransigence – and to be honest I've done just that at times. But their argument was not that this old petrol station – minutes from a tube station and next to a 20-storey tower block – was an invaluable ecological treasure, or even that it was doing anyone any good in its current state. It was that if they accepted a redrawing of the Green Belt boundary in this case, there would be no end to it. Greedy landowners and developers, egged on by politicians and housing campaigners like me, would move straight on to the next Green Belt site, and the next. To save the countryside from inevitable ruin, they honestly felt they had to resist every single change – no matter how reasonable. What Shaun calls 'bloody-minded defence' can be a rational response to a dysfunctional system.

Behind every angry campaign with a strong-but-simple message, there's almost always a group of people with a deep understanding of just how complex the issues really are – but who know that nuance and balanced debate won't cut it in the brutal competition for attention. So it's essential for campaigners to get out of the trenches every now and then, and kick a ball about in no-man's-land for a while. That is what this book does. There's always something to be learned from reaching out across the barricades – and more often than not the lesson is that the dividing lines aren't as stark as they seemed. As Shaun shows, CPRE was founded to promote good development as much as to preserve the countryside. And it remains committed to getting more homes built for those who need them – including in rural areas and sometimes on greenfield sites. In fact, rural areas desperately need more affordable homes if they are to be socially and economically sustainable. Social housing campaigners should find much to make common cause with in this book.

More uncomfortably, engaging with the other side of polarised debates also forces us to challenge our own shibboleths. That has certainly been my experience of working with Shaun, his colleagues at CPRE and others who are more instinctively concerned with the quality of the built and natural environment than with the quantity and price of homes. If we are honest, those of us who campaign for more homes have sometimes been less willing to recognise the importance of those homes being beautiful, in keeping with the local area, and in the most appropriate locations. This is our own failing, and one that the great founder of post-war social housing, Nye Bevan, resisted. His insistence that social homes in villages be built as cottages of local stone is a useful reminder that there is no contradiction between a revolution in social housing supply and the need to respect local traditions.

This important and timely book tackles these seemingly opposed positions head-on, and exposes just how inadequate each is for solving the housing crisis. The questions it asks are exactly those Shelter has been wrestling with for many years: how did our country come to be so bad at getting homes built? And how did house building get to be so unpopular?

The answers Shaun presents are not always easy to hear – for either side. But if you're upsetting all sides you must be doing something right, and for my money Shaun's diagnosis is spot on: we have lost the sense of planning as a positive, political act of shaping our neighbourhoods and our nation for the benefit of us all. The result is a system that frustrates local people and entrenches oppositional attitudes – and yet fails to give us the homes we need.

This book mounts a spirited defence of planning, in opposition to both knee-jerk NIMBYs and market fetishists. The planning system is a unique and peculiar set of institutions and policies – and the site of huge conflict. Repeated attempts to reduce the complexity and the cost of the planning system are doomed to fail, because the entire purpose of planning is to provide a rational, accountable framework for mediating intensely political conflicts over hugely valuable resources.

My own view is that this conflict is inherent in the unique nature of land. Land is finite, immobile, eternal and essential for all economic activity – and for life itself. While we assume exclusive ownership of many things in our lives, we also assume that we have the right to take an interest in how other people around us use their land. Add in the fact that most of our wealth is now tied up in the small bits of land we own, and it's unthinkable that land use could be anything other than a sensitive subject of political contestation. The question is how best to mediate that conflict and balance the competing interests of individuals, local communities and the nation as a whole.

For all his defence of the principle of good planning, Shaun is unsparing in his judgement of the realities of the current planning system as 'the worst of all worlds: a system that has lost public support but is so weak that it is unable to direct development to the most appropriate places or bring forward a sufficient supply of affordable land for development'. Fortunately he also offers a series of positive steps towards a better way of doing things.

It is simply not acceptable for those who own a nice house in a beautiful location to reject all development on the grounds that they don't need it and don't want it. But it's also not enough for those who do want more homes to duck the critical questions of where they should be built, what they should look like, and how they will impact the local community. Read this book with an open mind, and be ready to question your own assumptions. If we can overcome entrenched patterns of opposition, find new commonalities and forge new alliances, then perhaps we really could build enough houses *and* save the countryside.

Toby Lloyd, Shelter

Introduction

It is not intended to object to the reasonable use and development of rural areas: it is the abuse and bad development of such areas that requires restriction.... It is not intended that the CPRE shall be a merely negative force. It is part of its policy to promote suitable and harmonious development. (CPRE, 1926)

I joined the Campaign to Protect Rural England (CPRE) as its chief executive in 2004. My background was in the labour and cooperative movement. I was pro-housing and pro-people, so it was a shock to find that some seemed to regard me as England's 'Nimby-in-chief'. I had not intended to join a Nimby (Not In My Back Yard) organisation, and the more I got to know CPRE, the less I thought I had.

CPRE's staff tended to be liberal-left, as with most London-based non-governmental organisations (NGOs), and in the course of my 13 years with the organisation, more and more of them struggled with high property prices and the lousy treatment of renters. They were the 'jilted generation', but they were also strong defenders of the countryside. Nor did most CPRE members and supporters strike me as the selfish Nimbys of caricature. Many branch activists were involved in housing associations and housing charities, and they worried about where their children or grandchildren were going to live.

Of course, there are Nimbys in CPRE. There are Nimbys in developers' boardrooms and anywhere else you care to look. I never wanted CPRE to try to reclaim Nimbyism as a badge of honour because 'not in my back yard' implies that 'I don't care what happens in your back yard', a selfish attitude. However, wanting to improve and protect one's neighbourhood is a good thing: we could do with more of it. I do not know why someone fighting to keep a local school or hospital open is a community hero but someone fighting to protect a much-loved area of open space is condemned as a Nimby. Local people objecting to new housing are dismissed because they have a vested interest; however, developers and their allies have vested interests too.

We need more houses, but we also need more people willing to stand up for places they care about. Visit any part of the country and you will see ugly or jarring developments, from the relatively small-scale (unnecessary traffic signs, roadside billboards and street clutter of all sorts) to the out-of-scale shopping centres and distribution sheds that dominate the roads leading out of most towns. You will also see far too many anyplace housing estates squatting on the edge of historic towns, damaging their character and setting. As one developer told a CPRE seminar (Chatham House rules, I am afraid) "protestors aren't usually saying 'not in my back yard'; they're saying 'no shit in my back yard'".

In any case, CPRE's 43 county branches and 100-odd district groups cover large areas. Their aim is not to protect anyone's 'back yard', but to direct development to places where it will harm the countryside least and benefit it most. This was also the aim of the men and women (mostly men) who founded CPRE. They were remarkably open to the idea of change in the countryside provided that it was properly planned and, it must be said, provided that sophisticated and high-minded people like them helped guide it. 'This movement for preservation', David Matless (1998: 25) writes, 'entailed not a conservative protection of the old against the new but an attempt to plan a landscape simultaneously modern and traditional under the guidance of an expert public authority.'

The inspiration for CPRE's formation was a letter sent by Guy Dawber, President of the Royal Institute of British Architects, in January 1926 to 15 organisations with an interest in the future of rural England. This urged action to prevent its further 'destruction and disfigurement'. The need, he said, was twofold: 'the conservation of what is beautiful and interesting in our countryside and towns and villages; and the encouragement of the right type of development' (Waine and Hilliam, 2016: 46).

CPRE was formed (as the Council for the Preservation of Rural England) that December, with Dawber as Chair. From the start, it was less anti-development than pro-beauty: 'We have got to have new roads and bridges, new suburbs, new villages and perhaps new towns', said its first President, Lord Crawford, in a 1928 radio appeal. 'Our desire is that they shall be comely, and shall conform to modern requirements without injuring the ancient beauty of the land' (CPRE, 1928). The minutes of the inaugural meeting of CPRE Dorset in April 1937 record Crawford as saying:

> The Council were not against development; what they required and demanded was that the development should be on orderly and considered lines, by town and country planning, and not the mere haphazard aggregation of houses which did no credit to the past and which, before many generations had passed, would be an emphatic discredit to our day. What the Council stood for was orderly and well-considered development.

The planner Patrick Abercrombie, CPRE's first honorary Secretary, later Chair, was even more open to change. In his 1926 pamphlet *The preservation of rural England*, CPRE's foundation text, he wrote:

> There is no need to stem the inborn desire of the Englishman to live in the country or to have a garden. It should be possible for a stretch of country to absorb a large amount of building without losing its natural character or at any rate without destroying its beauty, though its character may be modified. (Abercrombie, 1926: 18)

The task was to see how much development the country could absorb 'without ceasing to be the country' (Abercrombie, 1926: 50). He concluded:

> It should be possible for a just balance to be struck between
> conservation and development: that certain parts must be
> preserved intact and inviolate but that others can, after suffering
> a change, bring forth something new but beautiful, provided a
> conscious effort is made. (Abercrombie, 1926: 56)

David Matless (1998: 44) characterises this approach as aiming to 'maintain rural distinctiveness through transformation'.

By the time I joined CPRE, it was clear that this pro-development spirit had been lost, together with any sense that development could be enhancing. CPRE was in the trenches. Our main campaigns were against house building, and this remained the case throughout my time as chief executive. We adopted an explicitly progressive vision for the countryside in 2026, our centenary year, a vision that embraced development and the idea that more people should live and work in the countryside (CPRE, 2009). However, day to day, our local groups were opposing house building at a time when far too few homes were being built across England to keep up with population growth. Why was this? How did our country come to be so bad at getting homes built? And how did house building get to be so unpopular?

This book explores these questions. It deals almost exclusively with England as the planning systems and housing cultures in the rest of the UK are so different. It makes the case for a stronger planning system and challenges those who advocate releasing more land or redrawing Green Belt boundaries as the way to get more homes built. It rehearses arguments that CPRE has been making for years and that are now beginning to be widely accepted, including by the government. The 2017 Housing White Paper, *Fixing our broken housing market* (DCLG, 2017a), was the first major government pronouncement on house building for at least 20 years not to start with an attack on planning. The recognition that it is the housing market, not the planning system, that is holding back development echoes the argument set out in CPRE's Housing Foresight report *Getting houses built* (Burroughs, 2015a): the major house builders who dominate the market have neither the will nor the capacity to build on the scale needed, whatever is done to the planning system. Indeed, Housing and Planning Minister Gavin Barwell was kind enough to tell CPRE: 'Any honest assessment of the Housing White Paper will quickly spot the marks of your influence' (Barwell, 2017).

The tone of the housing debate may have shifted but action is still lacking. Gavin Barwell lost his seat in the 2017 general election and, as I write, England has its 15th housing minister since 1997.[1] Countryside is still being needlessly lost or eroded as a direct result of national planning policy. Ministers either deny that this is happening or blame local decision-making, but it is a direct result of central government policy.

The first chapter sets out how politicians have been gulled by faith-based, ideologically predetermined anti-planning arguments from free-market think tanks such as Policy Exchange. While ministers were fixating on the planning system as a barrier to house building, they neglected to do the obvious thing: build houses.

This argumentative book also challenges my fellow countryside campaigners. Chapter Two sets out the scale of the housing crisis: too few homes; too many living in intolerable housing conditions; and growing and ultimately unsustainable inequality between those who own property (or whose parents own it) and those who do not and, as things stand, never will. We need to build more homes and we need to tackle inequality, which is intimately connected with housing. However, it should not be assumed that most new homes should be built in what are currently high-demand areas. There is a thin line between saying 'we need to build where people want to live' and stoking demand in those places.

Building more homes will require some sacrifice of greenfield land, though minimising its loss should be the aim of policy. CPRE has never opposed all development on greenfield land, but it is loath to propose sites for development. The poorly located, poorly executed developments that are now the norm across much of the country naturally stoke resistance. Chapter Three explores good and bad examples of house building in rural areas, what makes people oppose development and what might persuade them to support it. There is nothing wrong with saying 'no' to bad proposals, but it is not acceptable always to oppose new housing or to say airily 'put it all up north' or 'put it all on brownfield sites'. Conservationists should be readier to propose sites for development, including urban extensions and even new settlements. This can help protect towns and villages from the sort of haphazard and poor-quality development that is currently happening across England.

Chapter Four addresses those who doubt the value of landscapes or the importance of the Green Belt. Neither a short book nor a long walk in the countryside can convert the philistines, but I hope that I can at least help them understand why many people care so much. After that uplift, Chapter Five details the mess of the current planning system, and suggests how planning can win back a degree of legitimacy. Chapter Six draws out some of the policy proposals included in earlier chapters and makes some new ones.

The book is unapologetically pro-house building, but as chief executive of CPRE, I supported many campaigns against new housing. CPRE's principal role is to defend the countryside, not to act as a cheerleader for building in it. In a perfect world, any CPRE member might support developing this or that bit of countryside, particularly to provide new homes for those in need. However, we see a planning system that is skewed in favour of greenfield development. Those most noisily urging development in the countryside are rich and powerful, and stand to get richer from it. They are not building homes to meet housing need.

So, it is understandable that countryside campaigners say: 'Give them an inch and they'll take a mile. The only proven way to defend the countryside is bloody-minded defence.' As CPRE's then-President Max Hastings (2006) put it: 'the role of CPRE is to act as a burglar alarm on behalf of the countryside: to warn, to appeal, to point the spotlight, to cry from the rooftops about the consequences of thoughtless development.'

CPRE must continue to be a robust and sometimes unreasonable defender of the countryside. However, while this approach might succeed in holding back a deluge of damaging development in the

English countryside, it has not prevented its continued piecemeal erosion. Furthermore, it does not help answer the moral challenge posed by housing shortage. As well as opposing inappropriate development, conservationists should propose how to do developments better and where they should go. The aim should be both less damage to the countryside and more new houses. But to make this possible, policymakers must recognise that the current system needs radical change, both to improve the affordability of housing and to make it possible for groups like CPRE to engage more constructively.

Note

[1] In the January 2018 reshuffle, England got its 16th housing minister since 1997, the seventh since the Coalition government was elected in 2010.

ONE

How to think about housing and planning

Between 1951 and 1979, an average of 324,000 homes a year were built in the UK. The 1947 planning system did not prevent this, nor did protections such as Green Belts, national parks and Areas of Outstanding Natural Beauty (AONBs). The Campaign to Protect Rural England (CPRE) and other amenity groups were active and influential throughout the period.

House building was popular; it won votes. Addressing the housing shortage was the top priority in the 1945 general election, and the Labour manifesto promised to 'proceed with a housing programme with the maximum practical speed until every family in this island has a good standard of accommodation' (Lund, 2016: 1). The 1951 Conservative manifesto declared: 'Housing is the first of the social services…. a Conservative and Unionist Government will give housing a priority second only to national defence. Our target remains 300,000 houses a year.'[1] Churchill put the Tory programme more succinctly: 'housing and beef and not getting scuppered' (quoted in Addison, 1982 [1977]: 412).

Housing completions in England peaked in 1968 at 352,540 units, of which 143,680 were local authority homes, almost all built for social rent, and another 5,540 were housing association properties. Even allowing for the fact that demolitions were running at a high level, this is a striking contrast with the 140,660 homes completed in 2016, of which 2,080 were council homes and 23,939 were housing association properties, many for sale or market rent. More council homes were completed in 1968 than the total number of homes in any year since 2008.[2]

This chapter explores why we have failed to build enough new homes for almost 40 years. It begins by looking at the extraordinarily successful ideological assault on the planning system waged by a few influential free-market think tanks who blame it for our failure to build, distracting attention from the real causes. It then looks at four related issues that help explain why we need a new approach: the rise and fall of council housing; the economic model of the big developers; the rise and fall of the 'property-owning democracy'; and land values.

The chapter's five sections make a number of propositions.

1. The policy panacea of the free-market think tanks – liberalise planning policy in order to free more land for development – will not return Britain to pre-1979 levels of house building.
2. When the UK reliably built 200,000+ houses every year, local authorities built at least 100,000 of them. There needs to be a return to state-funded provision, but one that avoids the errors of the past. It is crazy to spend billions of pounds a year on housing benefit, subsidising private landlords and inflating house prices, rather than on building social housing.
3. The big house builders have neither the means nor desire to build on the scale needed.
4. Homes should not be seen principally as investments; governments should aim for house price stability or even a gradual fall in values. The government should stop suggesting that there is a straightforward relationship between supply and affordability.
5. The excessive cost of land restricts development, lowers quality and raises house prices. Land should not shoot up in value just because the state has granted planning permission. To help control land prices, we need a more confident state: more planning, not less.

The planning system and its enemies

> Even though nearly everyone lives or works in a town or city, somehow Britain has managed to retain its uncluttered rural areas. We take these for granted, but I consider them a huge achievement. I never thought I would one day be singing the praises of unassuming bureaucrats in town halls up and down the country, but it is almost entirely down to planning. Town and country planning ... is now the single most important factor affecting the look of Britain. And we meddle with it at our peril! (Pryor, 2010: 572–3)

When I joined CPRE in 2004, planning was widely blamed for the country's failure to build enough houses. The Treasury was intent on weakening it (it still is) and the government subjected the system to a series of reforms. However, it did not repudiate planning. Indeed, John Prescott was a strong supporter of strategic planning and advanced the brownfield agenda started by the previous Conservative government. The real intellectual attack on planning policy came from think tanks on the political Right. The most influential was Policy Exchange. Deeper into free-market la-la land were the Institute of Economic Affairs and the Adam Smith Institute (Alan Bennett's [2011] 'Adam Smith Institute for the Criminally Insane'). Their critique ignored the strong and very directive planning systems in countries like Germany and the Netherlands, and instead pined for US or Irish-style freedom to build.

We should not be surprised by the libertarians' hostility to planning. What is more surprising is that the planning system should have survived largely unscathed for 50 years after the Town and Country Planning Act 1947, almost as undisputed a part of the post-war settlement as the National Health Service (NHS). In many ways, it seems redolent of a world abandoned in 1979. Labour politicians in the post-war decades were enthusiasts for all sorts of planning, including economic planning. But the 1947 planning system, with its curtailment of property rights, was also embraced by the Conservatives.

For all her belief in free markets, Mrs Thatcher, a much more pragmatic politician than her epigones, largely respected the system. In a 1986 letter to CPRE's President, David Puttnam, she paid 'a warm tribute' to CPRE and welcomed the chance to 'set out clearly and explicitly this Government's commitment to the protection of the British countryside' (CPRE, 1986). It was, she said, 'vital to protect an inheritance of such unparalleled beauty and variety as our British countryside'; she boasted that the Green Belt had more than doubled in size since 1979 and she highlighted the government's priority of reusing previously developed land.

In truth, Mrs Thatcher's governments oversaw large-scale greenfield development and there was an undercurrent of anti-planning rhetoric from some ministers, notably, Nicholas Ridley. However, John Major's governments strengthened the planning system, seeing it as one of the most effective tools of environmental protection available. Conservative politicians might find planning irritating (many people who come up against planning restrictions find it irritating), but few saw it as conflicting with their ideology, if 'ideology' is the right word. Historically, British Conservatism has been a broad, flexible philosophy, more concerned with what works and wins elections than with ideology. Land-use planning was, and for the most part remains, a cross-party cause.

Indeed, the main authors of the Town and Country Planning Act 1947 were Conservatives. Much modified, the planning system recalls the post-war consensus that government exists to advance the public interest, not simply the interests of business, and that markets left to their own devices will not necessarily deliver satisfactory outcomes. This makes it a target for market ideologues and for those who do not want the public interest getting in the way of their own financial interests. As Hugh Ellis and Kate Henderson (2014: 9–10) put it, 'those who argue for the flexibility of the market are not really arguing against planning, they are arguing that it is their plan that should shape the future'.[3]

Land use is always controlled by someone and we should ask who would benefit from a significant weakening of the democratic planning system. It is a reasonable guess that those who pay for all the anti-planning reports pumped out by think tanks have something to gain. Unfortunately, we do not know who they are. The website whofundsyou.org rates think tanks from A to E according to their transparency. The main anti-planning think tanks are all rated 'E', meaning they provide 'no or negligible' information on their funders. However, it is always worth following the money, to the extent that you can (see Box 1.1).

Box 1.1: Follow the money

This is not an exposé of the house-building industry's bought influence, though someone should write one. A couple of hours' searching on the Internet throws up some information, but it is hard to find how much they pay for all those think tank reports that (conveniently) propose weakening the planning system.

There is more readily available information on political donations, principally to the Conservative Party. This became an issue in 2011 as the Coalition was drawing up the National Planning Policy Framework (NPPF), with its 'presumption in favour of sustainable development' (DCLG, 2012). The *Daily Telegraph* ran a series of articles exposing the extent of property company donations to the party. It revealed that they had donated £3.3 million over the previous three years, 'including large gifts from companies seeking to develop rural land' (*Daily Telegraph*, 2011). A group called the Conservative Planning Forum raised about £150,000 a year, charging members £2,500 to discuss policy and planning issues with senior MPs.

Presumably, donations continue, but it is hard to know what direct influence they have. What can be said with confidence is that party donors have very good access to ministers, and that these ministers have introduced policies that have made them a good deal of money. One of the most prominent developer-donors is Tony Gallagher of Gallagher Estates, a member of David Cameron's 'Chipping Norton set' and a dinner guest at Chequers. The Conservative blogger Guido Fawkes reported that Gallagher lent a helicopter to George Osborne so that he could attend a constituency fund-raising dinner in November 2015:

> Gallagher makes his money by buying up vast land banks and then developing them into houses or retail parks. So he has directly benefited from Osborne's "*we are the builders*" development drive. Not to mention the liberalisation of planning laws to make property development easier.

Gallagher's companies own 35,000 house-building plots throughout the UK, so an £8,000 chopper is a good investment to keep the housing-bubble inflating Chancellor sweet.[4]

In July 2017, a Channel 4 Dispatches documentary reported that another of Gallagher's companies had won a battle to halve the number of affordable homes on the Northstowe development in Cambridgeshire, and remove a restriction on minimum room sizes. It reported that he had donated £1.25 million to the Conservative Party and was a member of its Leader's Group, which gives access to the prime minister.[5]

There is no clear causal link between Gallagher's donations and access to senior ministers, on the one hand, and the policies that benefit his business (and enable the donations), on the other. Nor is there any clear causal link between John Bloor's (of Bloor Homes) £400,000 donation to the Conservative Party and his use of the government's Help to Buy scheme to sell leasehold properties,[6] or his firm's building on land removed from the Green Belt,[7] or (as reported by Dispatches) its success in reducing by three quarters the target for affordable homes in a development in Northamptonshire.

Nor is there any clear causal link in the many other cases one can find on the Internet or in *Private Eye*. I suspect that these developers would donate to the Conservative Party in any case, and I do not think that the government was consciously influenced by donations when it introduced policies that happened to benefit its donors. The concern is not so much about integrity, as transparency and fairness. The dinners and donor events certainly make developer-friendly policies more likely, and those campaigning for affordable housing or countryside protection simply cannot compete with this access.

There are eye-watering sums of money to be made through house building, particularly if planning requirements can be weakened. There are also respectable arguments for planning reform and for releasing more greenfield land for development. These should be considered on their merits and I do not suggest that everyone making them is venal. But when you hear ministers and MPs talking about the planning straitjacket and the need for liberalisation, it is worth wondering who they have been chatting to at a party fund-raiser. Furthermore, when you read a report or article condemning red tape or arguing that we need to build on the Green Belt, think about who paid for it and what they have to gain.

For a couple of years after I joined CPRE, our spat with the anti-planning think tanks was an enjoyable sideshow. The Labour government did not seem too influenced and the Conservative opposition did not want to alienate its core supporters in the shires. It was gratifying (if nonsense) to have Policy Exchange write: 'It would be no exaggeration to say that planning policy has come to be controlled by the vociferous Campaign to Protect Rural England' (Evans and Hartwich, 2006: 14), In *Policy-based evidence making* (CPRE, 2006), we analysed three Policy Exchange reports and one from the Adam Smith Institute. The Adam Smith Institute report called for the abolition of the planning system, which was at least honest and intellectually consistent. A recurring line from our report, 'what planet are they on?', was later used by the Policy Exchange to promote its reports.

The think-tankers, many of them the sort of young men who would have grown up with posters of Mrs Thatcher on their bedroom walls, just hated planning. For Alex Morton (2011: 11), it was 'a dysfunctional ... system created by the post war Labour government as part of a new and socialist command economy'. Alan W. Evans and Oliver Marc Hartwich (2005: 14) said of the introduction of the plan-led system in 1990:

> It is a paradox to be savoured that a year after the Berlin Wall came down, whilst the Soviet economy and its satellites were collapsing, a Conservative government should have enforced a system of Soviet-style central planning for the provision of housing in Britain.

In 2013, James (now Lord) O'Shaughnessy recalled how, as deputy director of Policy Exchange from 2007 to 2010:

> I commissioned a series of reports that highlighted the dreadful impact of the under-supply of housing that has resulted from our Soviet-style planning system (just think about the meaning of the

term 'planning', and how Conservatives reject its effectiveness in almost every sphere apart from housing). (O'Shaughnessy, 2013: 127–8)

Planning, he said, 'is exactly this kind of cartel that the most successful Conservative leaders have taken on' (O'Shaughnessy, 2013: 128). O'Shaughnessy was David Cameron's first head of policy in the Coalition government.

In time, the 'war on planning', a steady stream of reports supported by seminars, newspaper articles and private lunches and dinners, began to have an impact. Planning came to be widely blamed for the country's failure to build enough homes and, more generally, for holding back economic development. David Cameron called planning officers the "enemies of enterprise". Eric Pickles described the English planning system as the last outpost of Albanian Communism. George Osborne mused wistfully to Andrew Marr about the speed with which development is agreed in China (he blamed planning rather than democracy for our relative slowness). In the run-up to the planning reforms of 2012, politicians of all parties, supported by newspaper commentators, talked of planning as a brake on house building and economic growth, not as something vital to business certainty and the quality of development.

The NPPF was clearly influenced by this anti-planning drumbeat. The original intention was good, but the final document had the Chancellor's fingerprints all over it. His aim was to stop people stopping development. Paragraph 14 of the NPPF states that at its heart is 'a presumption in favour of sustainable development, which should be seen as a golden thread running through both plan-making and decision-making' (DCLG, 2012). The word 'sustainable' was window dressing. CPRE, the National Trust and the *Daily Telegraph* fought a long and partly successful campaign to improve the NPPF, but after its introduction, the opponents of planning had even greater influence.

In November 2012, Nick Boles was appointed as planning (or anti-planning) minister. He had previously condemned 'our sclerotic planning system' for making the process of turning agricultural land into buildings (apparently an unequivocally good thing) 'an exercise of Gothic complexity and horrifying cost'. He wanted a 'reassertion of the rights of property owners to develop as they see fit, without unnecessary interference by any planning authority'. This would 'require a wholesale reduction in the burden of regulation that controls what buildings you can build, where you can build them and how' (Boles, 2010: 18–19). In November 2010, he said that he did not believe that planning could work; he preferred a degree of chaos (quoted in *The Observer*, 2010).

I remember debating with Boles on the Today programme when he was the founder director of Policy Exchange and the think tank had brought out one of its first anti-planning reports. We had a friendly chat and I thought that he was just enjoying making a stir. I wish I had taken him more seriously. "Builder Boles", as Max Hastings called him, wound up the Conservative heartlands, provoked opposition even to reasonable development proposals and helped pay my salary. CPRE's fund-raisers knew him as "the gift that keeps on giving"; donations came in every time he made a speech or gave an interview as planning minister. However, I doubt that the aggro he generated resulted in a single extra home being built.

The great Policy Exchange land-use experiment got another boost in 2013 when Alex Morton, the energetic author of umpteen Policy Exchange reports on housing and planning, became the prime minister's special adviser. It was clear that ministers from David Cameron down viewed planning liberalisation as the way to get more houses built. However, successive planning reforms over successive governments have had little impact on supply. If anything, there has been a temporary dip after each reform as everyone gets used to the new system. The principal cause of our failure to build enough houses is not planning. It should have been obvious to anyone looking at the figures: the state has stopped building houses.

Council housing

"I think, frankly, that the only way you're going to get low-paid workers a proper house and a proper living is to build bloody council houses at an affordable price." (Participant at CPRE Oxfordshire focus group, May 2017)

It is extraordinary that so many clever people could look at our failure to build enough homes and conclude that planning must be to blame, rather than the collapse in council house building. The assumption seems to have been that we live in a market age so there has to be a market solution to the housing challenge: liberalisation and then more liberalisation when the liberalisation fails to deliver. The advocates of planning liberalisation ignored the fact that for 30 years after the Second World War, when more than 200,000 homes were built every year in the UK, local authorities built at least 100,000 of them. Between 1951 and 1979, 48% of new homes were built for social rent. After 1979, local authorities virtually ceased to build and neither the private nor housing association sectors increased their output enough to make up the shortfall. Thus, the housing crisis.

Now, at last, there is growing agreement across all parties that the private sector will get nowhere near to delivering the homes the country needs, however permissive the planning system. It has been fascinating over the last couple of years to observe a growing consensus that we need a more active state and a big increase in social housing. As Martin Crookston (2014: 18) says of post-war housing delivery: 'The very high annual home-building rate of these years was primarily a product of the political determination to make it happen.' Politicians were determined to see houses built, so they got on and built them. Similar political determination is needed now.

Figure 1.1: Permanent dwellings completed by tenure, 1946–2016

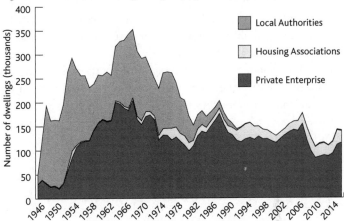

Source: Department for Communities and Local Government (DCLG): Table 244 –
permanent dwellings started and completed, by tenure, England, historical calendar
year series. Available at: www.gov.uk/government/statistical-data-sets/live-tables-on-
house-building

Figure 1.2: Council housing as a percentage of all house building, 1946–2016

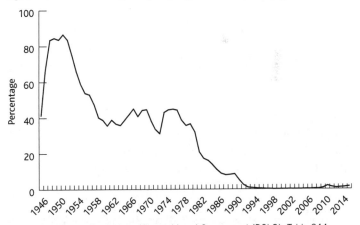

Source: Department for Communities and Local Government (DCLG): Table 244 –
permanent dwellings started and completed, by tenure, England, historical calendar
year series. Available at: www.gov.uk/government/statistical-data-sets/live-tables-on-
house-building

The greater willingness in the last couple of years to talk about market failure owes a good deal to the inescapable evidence that outsourcing the state's responsibility for housing ('the first of the social services') has failed. The impact of failed policies has now spread beyond the poor and the young to the middle class and middle aged. However, the change is quite recent. In the 2015 general election, all the main parties agreed that more homes should be built (they always do) but the main point of controversy was the Conservative pledge to sell off housing association homes in order to bolster home ownership. Responsibility for the failure to build enough houses was blamed on Nimbys, profit-maximising private businesses for behaving like profit-maximising private businesses and, of course, the planning system. There was little analysis of the failure of the Coalition's response to the housing crisis, nicely summarised by James Meek as 'to try to make it worse'.

> It is taking steps to increase house prices, without taking steps to increase supply. The coalition's two most explicit interventions in the housing market have been to restrict supply and raise prices: the first when it cut, by two thirds, the grant given to housing associations to build new homes, and the second with its mocking parody of Right to Buy, 'Help to Buy', offering already well-off people cheap loans to overbid for overpriced houses they couldn't otherwise afford. (Meek, 2014)

In the 2017 general election, all parties promised a greater role for the state and more social housing, a remarkable change in just two years. The evidence helped change thinking, but there was also a battle of ideas. CPRE played its part in this. For years, we were one of the few mainstream bodies telling governments to stop crying crocodile tears about undersupply and instead build the new homes that they said they wanted. However, we did so rather quietly, partly because of our charitable remit, partly because, like most organisations, we tended to work within the agenda set by the government. It is a brave organisation that devotes resources to campaigns when no one is listening. Building council houses was as beyond the pale for New Labour as for the Conservatives: even in the 2010 election, the party only proposed to let local authorities build up to 10,000 council homes a year by the end of the Parliament. But a campaign group should not just accept that good ideas are out of the range of practical politics. Its job is also to shift paradigms and alter the frames within which politics is discussed. That is something think tanks do well.

When I first joined CPRE, Shelter was campaigning for a step change in the supply of market housing, rather than for social housing. The National Housing Federation (NHF), the trade body for housing associations, seemed keener to attack the Green Belt (a profitable area for development whether you are a private builder or a housing association) than to make the case for funding social housing. Indeed, many of the groups and commentators expressing outrage on behalf of the 'priced out' seemed keener to attack the Green Belt than to support public house building. In retrospect, it seems bizarre that everyone quarrelled about where to build and what targets to set, without asking more insistently who was going to build the houses and for whom.

Gradually, however, the tide of thinking has turned. Ideas ultimately drive politics. In recent years, think tanks have had a far greater impact over policy than most campaign groups. As Keynes almost said, 'madmen in authority, who hear voices in the air, are distilling their frenzy from some think tank scribbler of a few years back'. Having spent much of my time at CPRE reacting to the fallout from some half-baked Policy Exchange pamphlet of several years before, early in 2014 we appointed a new post, a sort of in-house think-tanker tasked with proposing countryside-friendly ways of building more houses. Gradually, our Housing Foresight reports began to have an impact, but plenty of others were thinking along the same lines. Ministers became increasingly critical of the private sector's slowness in building out its planning permissions. Labour policy was also changing. Its 2014 Lyons housing review recommended more support for housing associations and a bigger (though still modest) role for councils in building new homes (Lyons, 2014: 30).

Shelter and the centre-right think tank Civitas were particularly influential and I borrow from their reports throughout this book. When Shelter and CPRE are able to say much the same thing (along with other pro-housing organisations such as the Town and Country Planning Association), you know that a powerful consensus is developing. At the autumn 2017 party conferences, Shelter and CPRE held joint fringe meetings, a real breakthrough. Furthermore, as the argument took hold that the private sector will never build enough and the public sector has to build more, Policy Exchange gradually stopped saying much about housing and planning, another good result.[8]

CPRE did not specifically campaign for more council house building, but some nostalgia for the council house era is forgivable. By 1979, almost half the population lived in a council home and the British people had never been so well housed: securely, affordably and, for the most part, with plenty of space. Compared with the slums they replaced, council homes were a blessing, and so they seem compared with what has come since, at least for those unable to buy: insecure tenure, high rents and the hounding of those social tenants deemed to occupy too much space or earn too much money to deserve social housing.

However, it is impossible to turn the clock back. Britain has changed dramatically since 1979, culturally and economically, and it would be neither feasible nor desirable to return to the era of mass council building. As well as acknowledging the huge contribution made by council housing, it is important to remember why it fell out of favour. Local authorities gave millions of people the best homes that they had ever lived in. They were often better than private sector homes in terms of space and build quality. But there was also widespread dissatisfaction, particularly with high-rise flats. Too often, at least after Nye Bevan's tenure as housing minister (see Box 1.2), quality came second to speed of delivery.

Box 1.2: Nye Bevan: the path abandoned

Aneurin Bevan is the only housing minister consciously to have sacrificed numbers to quality, and the Labour Party paid an electoral price. It is worth a diversion to look at the five years Bevan was in charge of housing because the period throws an interesting light on some of the issues we face now.

The 1930s saw a house-building boom for which, as Bevan's biographer Michael Foot (1975: 61) acknowledges, 'unfettered private enterprise was primarily responsible'. Bevan's decision to put local authorities in charge of housing delivery, under his direction, was justified on the grounds that the conditions underpinning the pre-war boom were absent in 1945: given the post-war scarcity of builders and building materials, putting private firms in charge would not deliver the number of homes the country needed. 'If we are to plan', Bevan said, 'we have to plan with plannable instruments, and the speculative builder, by his very nature, is not a plannable instrument' (*Hansard*, 6 March 1946, HC vol 420, col 451).

Beyond this, Bevan believed that the private sector would neither deliver good-quality homes and places, nor help those most in need. He despised the quality of much interwar house building: 'You only have to look at the fretful fronts stretching along the great roads leading from London ... to see the monstrous crimes committed against aesthetics by ... private speculators in house building' (*Hansard*, 17 October 1945, HC vol 414, col 1223). Conservative MPs, he noted:

> do not live in those houses, or near them. They always select the most delectable parts of the country to live in, and they do not live in the areas where they let loose the speculative builder.... If I go down in history for nothing else, I will go down at least as a barrier between the beauty of Great Britain and the speculative builder who has done so much to destroy it. (*Hansard*, 13 March 1950, HC vol 472, col 862)

It was important to Bevan that council homes were at least as good as private homes: 'While we shall be judged for a year or two by the *number* of houses we build', Bevan said, 'we shall be judged in ten years' time by the *type* of houses we build' (Foot, 1975: 80, emphases in original). To cut standards, he said, would be:

> a cruel thing to do. After all, people will have to live in and among these houses for many years. Enough damage has already been done to the face of England by irresponsible people. If we have to wait a little longer, that will be far better than doing ugly things now and regretting them for the rest of our lives. (Foot, 1975: 78)

However, standards were cut as soon as he left office in 1950.

One policy of which Bevan was particularly proud was a subsidy for councils to build in local stone: 'Of all the monuments left behind him', Foot (1975: 79–80) recalls, 'the lovely post-war cottages in the Cotswolds, suited to the surrounding countryside, were among those of which he was proudest.' Securing Treasury agreement was a surprising achievement but the Chancellor, Sir Stafford Cripps, had a personal interest. Before the war, he had paid to ensure that council houses in his (and later my) home village of Filkins in Oxfordshire were built in Cotswold stone, with slate roofs from the local quarry (which, conveniently, he owned). The council houses that Cripps subsidised became the first in the country to be Grade II listed, and Filkins's post-war council houses were also built of local stone (Swinford, 1987: 104, 111). How much easier it would be to get villages to accept new housing today if similar care was taken over their appearance.

As well as ensuring their quality, Bevan wanted council houses to be integrated with the wider community, saying:

> We should try to introduce in our modern villages and towns what was always the lovely feature of English and Welsh villages, where the doctor, the grocer, the butcher and the farm labourer all lived in the same street. I believe that is essential for the full life of a citizen ... to see the living tapestry of a mixed community. (Foot, 1975: 76)

One last feature of Bevan's time as housing minister is worth recalling, his passion for housing the least well off. This was personal. As he told the House of Commons in March 1950, 'I do not need to be told here about what are the consequences of living in bad houses. I was born in a bad house' (*Hansard*, 13 March 1950, HC vol 472, col 868). Five years earlier, he declared that 'the housing problem for the lower income groups in this country has not been solved since the industrial revolution'. Before the war, the problem had been largely solved for higher-income groups by speculative builders supported by easy finance. 'We propose to start at the other end. We propose to start to solve, first, the housing difficulties of the lower income groups' (*Hansard*, 17 October 1945, HC vol 414, col 1222).

The idea that governments should give the highest priority to housing those most in need, rather than boosting home ownership, became deeply unfashionable after 1979. Bevan made the case with characteristic vigour. The government would not 'pour out public money to private enterprise ... in order to build houses to sell'. Scarce labour and building materials would be used 'for those who need houses, and not for those who can buy them'. To the opposition, proposing that private enterprise would solve the housing shortage ('the old Tory claptrap'), he said: 'The only remedy they have for every social problem is to enable private enterprise to suck at the teats of the State' (*Hansard*, 6 March 1946, HC vol 420, col 453).

Considering the various markets solutions to tackling the housing shortage that we have tried over the last 30 or 40 years, and the subsidies for home ownership that have lasted even longer, I can only wish I had Bevan's eloquence. Since the housing crash of 2008, the state has thrown money at the house builders, first to keep them afloat, then in an attempt to persuade them to build. Schemes such as Help to Buy (to which the Chancellor committed another £10 billion in 2017) have contributed less to housing output than to handsome dividend payments and scandalous executive pay settlements (such as a whopping £600 million for the Persimmon executive team).[9] Private enterprise is sucking ever harder at the teats of the state.

Large-scale council estates, however good the quality of the homes, were easy to stigmatise: 'You only have to say the word "estates" for someone to infer a vast amount of meaning from it', says Lynsey Hanley (2007: 20). 'It's a bruise in the form of a word.'[10] After Bevan left office, space, build and design standards were rapidly weakened. Worst of all were the tower blocks. Between 1945 and 1950, 10.5% of the local authority homes built were flats. By Harold Wilson's second term as prime minister (1966–70), the figure was just over half, rising to 90% in inner cities. Council high-rises were among the many 'great planning disasters' that helped give planning a bad name and undermine the idea that planners could be trusted to represent the interests and values of society. They arose from a target-driven policy culture that emphasised quantity, not quality – a familiar tale.

There was no popular rush to defend council housing against the Right to Buy, introduced by Mrs Thatcher's 1979 government. The policy proved so popular that by the 1987 election, Labour had dropped its opposition provided that the sale receipts were used to build new council homes. The New Labour government elected in 1997 wanted nothing to do with council housing. As Conservative ministers like to point out, fewer council homes were built in its 13 years in office than in the five years of the Coalition. Nor did it invest heavily in other forms of social housing. New Labour evolved a workable and cost-effective model for investing in 'registered social landlords' (dismantled by the Coalition) but put relatively little money in.

Rather than building, Labour focused on improving the existing stock, though it seemed oddly reluctant to take credit for the £40 billion Decent Homes Programme. This was needed because, in Nick Raynsford's (2016: 55) words, 'a combination of poor design, construction defects and unsatisfactory management and maintenance [had] led to the physical decline ... of substantial numbers of council estates'. I canvassed on many such estates in the 1980s and 1990s and never felt further from the New Jerusalem. Between 2000 and 2010, the government forced the transfer of 770,340 council homes to specially created housing associations, believing that they would be better landlords and in order to get social housing off the public balance sheet (Lund, 2016: 169). What public money there was for house building went to housing associations, and they built no more than they had under John Major's government. Just over 30,000 housing association homes were completed in England in both 1994 and 1995; the highest total in Labour's 13 years in office was 26,990 in 2009.

The Right to Buy, combined with the non-replacement of sold council homes, resulted in a significant reduction in the social housing stock. At least 2.7 million council, housing association and new town homes were sold to their tenants between 1980 and 2015, just over 1.9 million of them in England (Murie, 2016: 66–7). The boon for many of the purchasers should not be dismissed too lightly. Lynsey Hanley (2007: 142), a sceptic, notes that most of those who bought:

> would have acquired the first assets they or their families had ever owned. For the first time, they had wealth that could be passed on to their children. At first, it's hard to think of this as being a bad thing.

However, for all that it undoubtedly benefited hundreds of thousands of individuals and families, the Right to Buy also had damaging consequences, not only in terms of reducing the stock of social housing (a particular concern in rural areas: see Chapter four), but also for the politics of housing (see later). Compared with 30 years ago, more voters have an interest in keeping up house prices and there is a much smaller constituency of voters with an interest in social housing. Political priorities reflect this change, with a greater focus on pleasing homeowners. This remains the case even as the numbers of homeowners decline and politicians give more attention to rental housing. At the 2017 Conservative Party conference, Theresa May promised £2 billion for social housing, enough to build around 5,000 council homes a year; however, she announced another £10 billion for Help to Buy in order to enable young voters to get on the 'housing ladder'.

Alongside the sale and non-replacement of council house stock came what Nick Raynsford (2016: 37–52) calls 'the irresistible rise of housing benefit'. What the country used to spend on building new homes to let at below-market rents it now spends subsidising higher levels of rent. Ironically, much of the money ends up in the pockets of the landlords of former council homes. Alan Murie (2016: 104–7) calculates that 30–40% of former Right to Buy properties are now in the private rented sector. The number of recipients of housing benefit has not varied greatly in the last 30 years, but the cost has more than tripled, from £7.9 billion in 1985/86 to £24.4 billion in 2015/16 (adjusted for inflation) (Raynsford, 2016: 43). Put another way:

> whereas in 1975 more than 80% of housing subsidies were supply-side subsidies to promote the construction of social homes, by 2000 more than 85% of housing subsidies were on the demand side aimed at helping individual tenants pay the required rent. (Ryan-Collins et al, 2017: 89)

Switching state support from building homes to subsidising rents, from bricks to benefits, must surely rank among the biggest 'blunders of our governments' of the post-war era.[11] No government would want to start from here. Nearly one in five households depends on housing benefit, and finding money for house building while also supporting rents will not be easy. One way round the problem is to allow councils to borrow to build. Under European Union (EU) rules, local authority investment in housing does not count as public debt; under Treasury rules, it does. If they were allowed to do so, local authorities would be able to borrow at low interest rates and make a decent long-term return from council housing, provided they were not forced to sell it too quickly and at too great a loss. The UK government should change its fiscal rules (Ryan-Collins et al, 2017: 219–21).

A substantial programme of publicly funded house building, whether by councils or housing associations, would also support private sector output, as Ryan-Collins et al (2017: 83–4) explain:

> The years in which the state built most were also those in which the market built most, suggesting that state supply caused little if any crowding out of private investment. If anything, the opposite was true, as relatively small regional and local building firms were able to take contracts to build homes for the council while financing a few speculative homes for sale themselves.

State supply helps keep small builders in business when the market for private homes is flat. This counter-cyclical function is particularly important as with each downturn, the house-building industry becomes concentrated in fewer, larger firms. When the market recovers, each new peak in supply is lower than the last. It is crucial to nurture smaller firms, and public investment in house building is one way of doing so (Ryan-Collins et al, 2017: 96).

Figure 1.3 shows the decline in new builds for social rent from 39,560 homes in 2010/11 (the highest rate since 1996/97) to just 6,800 in 2015/16. Provisional figures published by DCLG in November 2017 suggest that only 5,380 homes for social rent were completed in 2016/17. Ostensibly, the Coalition switched subsidies from social housing to housing for 'affordable rent', defined as 80% of market rent, but only 16,550 homes were built for affordable rent in 2015/16, increasing to 24,350 in 2016/17. 'Affordable rent' is, in any case, a misnomer. For whom is 80% of market rent affordable in a property hotspot? Furthermore, if, as the government acknowledges, the housing market is 'broken', why should we measure rents against this broken market? As John Lanchester (2017) wryly notes, 'even the alternative to the market defers to the market'.

Figure 1.3: Additional affordable homes for social rent, England

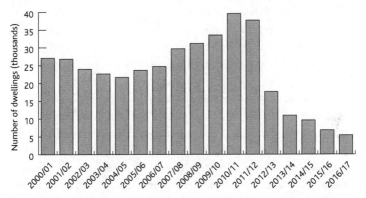

Source: DCLG: Live Tables. Table 1000: Additional affordable homes provided by type of scheme, England. Available at: https://www.gov.uk/government/statistical-data-sets/live-tables-on-affordable-housing-supply

We have had a long period of historically low interest rates, presenting a golden opportunity for a programme of public house building. But public institutions have either been unwilling to borrow to build (central government) or barred from doing so (local government). So the housing crisis continues, with more debate and rhetoric than action.

The housing market

It is not, however, necessary to aim to build 100,000 council homes a year. When targets dominate housing policy, the result is poor-quality design, shoddy construction and places you would not want to live in. We learnt that lesson with council house building in the 1950s and 1960s, and we should learn it again from the way target-driven policies have worked in the last few years. We should build more houses, but we should also give a high priority to creating good homes and places in which to live. So, rather than new mass council estates, we need a mix of providers – councils, housing associations, housing cooperatives and private landlords – as well as shared ownership and owner-occupation.

The big firms that dominate the market have a major role to play in building the homes the country needs. But they will not build enough new homes and they will not build enough homes that are affordable for those most in need. Around 15 firms build half the country's new homes. They build the number of homes they want to build and that they think the market will support. If they are allowed to build them in the countryside, they will do so, but that does not mean that they will build more homes in total. They do not lack land on which to build. In addition to their disclosed land banks with planning permission, developers are estimated to control around four times more land in the form of shadow land banks where they have confidential option deals with landowners (Ryan-Collins et al, 2017: 96–7). In addition, as CPRE has demonstrated, there is enough suitable brownfield land in England for at least a million new homes (see Chapter Five) (Sinnett et al, 2014; CPRE, 2016).

Read the annual and half-yearly reports of any of the volume house builders and two things become clear. First, to quote Wimpey's 2012 annual report, they 'prioritise both short and long term margin performance ahead of volume growth' (Griffith and Jefferys, 2013). In other words, private house builders are not social enterprises. Their aim is to make as much profit as possible and they maximise their profits by building fewer, rather than more, houses. Second, they work on high margins, generally over 20%.

House builders complain about planning, and the system is no doubt slower and more irksome than they would wish. That is to be expected. A planning system that never refused a development or which failed to ask serious questions of developers would not be worth having. However, when they get planning permission, the big builders are in no hurry to build. They constantly complain about slow processes but total output is largely in their hands. I have always found it surprising that newspapers (particularly the *Financial Times*) accept so unquestioningly the house builders' line that planning is to blame for low output. They would say that, wouldn't they? As the then Housing Minister, Gavin Barwell (2017), pointed out in his CPRE lecture: 'There's a large and growing gap between homes being granted planning permission and homes being started. And people can't live in a planning permission.'

All this was the subject of CPRE's fourth Housing Foresight report in June 2015, *Getting houses built: How to accelerate the delivery of new housing* (Burroughs, 2015a), which examined the business model of the large builders. House builders tend to deny that they deliberately restrict supply. They argue that slow build-out rates are down to a shortage of materials and labour, a problem set to get worse if the government is serious about getting immigration down to the tens of thousands. The scandal over poorly finished homes certainly suggests that the big builders would find it hard to speed up supply even if they wanted to. But whatever the reasons, it is clear that the big builders will not build enough new homes.

They have pleaded for planning liberalisation, weaker building standards, relaxations on design quality and an end to zero-carbon homes, and they have been given most of what they asked for. The beneficiaries of this government generosity have been their shareholders and executives, not those in housing need. This should surprise no one, and it is extraordinary that governments have for so long fallen for the house builders' 'give us the tools and we will finish the job' rhetoric. As the *Callcutt review of housing delivery* pointed out in 2007: 'Housebuilders are not in the business of serving the public interest, except incidentally. Their primary concern is to deliver profits for their investors.... Housebuilding executives are answerable to their investors, not to Ministers or the wider public' (Callcutt Review, 2007).

This is pretty obvious. The idea that, left to itself, the market will provide enough good-quality, affordable homes is a fantasy of think tank ideologues. Even where planning is weak and land plentiful, there are housing shortages. It was ever thus. Daniel Bentley of the centre-right think tank Civitas has analysed the decades leading up to 1914, the last time Britain had a wholly free market in house building, with no planning system and few or no completions from the public sector. A boom in the 1890s was followed by a long slump. House prices fell but rents remained high, forcing more families to share lodgings. The reasons for the slump are complex, but the clear conclusion of politicians of all parties was that, to quote Lloyd George, 'you cannot provide houses in this country by private enterprise' (Bentley, 2017: 30). It was, says Bentley, precisely the failings of the free market in this period that led to growing state involvement in housing in the decades after the First World War (Bentley, 2017).

Housing is often spoken of as a national emergency, but it is not treated as an emergency. Business as usual prevails.

- Alconbury Weald in Cambridgeshire, a large and in many ways exemplary development on a former Royal Air Force base, is being built almost entirely for private ownership. There are no social houses. The house builders expect to build at a rate of about one house a week, meaning that a developer's allocation of 200 homes will take four years to complete (Spiers, 2016).
- There are four other large, long-term developments in Cambridgeshire, in addition to significant building in and around Cambridge and Peterborough. CPRE Cambridgeshire broadly supports four of the new settlements, Alconbury Weald, Northstowe, Waterbeach (715 acres of ex-Ministry of Defence land just three miles north of Cambridge) and Cambourne. However, in spite of all this planned development in a booming county, Cambridgeshire councils are losing planning appeals. The developments are being built out slowly, by traditional construction methods, for private sale. Crisis, what crisis? One person's housing crisis is another person's economic opportunity.
- Ebbsfleet in Kent is a superbly situated site. It is near the M2, M25 and Dartford Crossing, 20 minutes from London St Pancras and less than three hours from Paris and Brussels by high-speed train.

Yet, at current building rates, it will take a century to complete the planned 15,000 homes.

Other large developments are being built out equally slowly. Some of this is down to a lack of infrastructure, some to the economic model of the house builders. However, it is odd when people see large sites developed at such a stately pace and conclude that the solution is not to speed up development, but to build in the Green Belt. The major house builders need to be put under more pressure. They have taken the government and their customers for a ride. Too often, they treat leaseholders scandalously, build shoddy homes and give almost no attention to place making.

But it would be naive to rely on a few private firms to build the homes that the country needs. The market needs new players. Local authorities have a role to play. So do housing associations, which completed 38,000 homes in 2016/17, including 4,800 for social rent (National Housing Federation, 2017b). They aim to increase output to 120,000 homes a year, with half for sale and half for rent. Some large housing associations seem to have mislaid their social mission, but at least they are building houses.

There should be a bigger role for custom-built housing, modern methods of construction and small builders. As recently as 1988, small- and medium-sized builders (those building up to 1,000 homes a year) were responsible for 40% of new homes built in England and Wales. They now build 12%, and their market share is falling (Home Builders Federation, 2017: 6). Small builders need easier access to finance, and more can be done to identify the sort of small, brownfield sites that do not interest the big builders.

In the Netherlands, the number of custom-built homes doubled in three years. The UK Right to Build Task Force aims to learn from this example. Its Chair, Richard Bacon MP, sees potential for an extra 60,000 units a year in the UK (Bacon, 2017: 15). This is a genuinely exciting area, full of potential. When I visited the Netherlands in 2016 with Igloo Regeneration, I was blown away by what I saw. The developments were high-density, but the houses were generally four storeys tall and spacious. The frames were factory built, but the details in the design gave them character and individuality. They were completed in a fraction of the time it takes to build houses in the UK. One small, ex-industrial site on the outskirts of Amsterdam was being quickly transformed by a couple of dozen custom-built homes.

The government should stop relying on the big builders to supply the homes that the country needs. Having correctly identified that the housing market is 'broken', it must step up its efforts to diversify the market. There is no use in blaming planning for our failure to build enough homes if we do not have the institutions able and willing to build on the scale needed.

The politics of housing

If housing politics was just about increasing supply, it would be easier, if not entirely easy. However, it is greatly complicated by the wealth tied up in housing. The marginalisation of social housing has made home ownership increasingly important politically. Homeowners have a big financial interest in protecting their assets, and they vote. Renters are less likely to vote, not least because they are six times more likely than owner-occupiers to move house within a year. The snap 2017 election threw a spotlight on this issue. Two million renters who were eligible to vote had moved house since the EU referendum less than a year before.[12] Many will have failed to get on the electoral register in their new homes.

Since 1979, all governments have aimed to increase home ownership and make it the tenure of choice. Home ownership has many benefits, but houses are now too often seen, in Nye Bevan's words, 'as commodities to be bought and sold' (quoted in Lund, 2016: 147). Homeowners like to see the value of their asset appreciate, and whatever concern they may express about affordability, governments always seem happy to see house price inflation.

- Rising house prices win elections.
- Tax receipts from a booming property market fund government programmes; New Labour's investment in public services (though not house building) was partly funded from stamp duty and other property taxes that rose as house prices increased.
- A huge amount of personal and national wealth is now tied up in housing. Investment in property and borrowing against property has been described as a form of 'privatised Keynesianism' (Ryan-Collins et al, 2017: 146). In January 2017, Savills valued the UK's housing stock at £6.8 trillion, 3.65 times Britain's gross domestic product (GDP). Private housing equity was worth £5 trillion, or £5,000,000,000,000.[13] No government could afford a sudden drop in property values.

The incompatibility of constant house price inflation with notions of a property-owning democracy is becoming ever clearer. Home ownership peaked in 2003 and owner-occupation with a mortgage in 1999 (Ryan-Collins et al, 2017: 101, 178). Rising prices have choked off demand from first-time buyers. The statistics are well-rehearsed and sobering.

- The affordability ratio of median houses to median incomes for England as a whole rose from 3.54 in 1997 to 7.63 in 2015 (Bowie, 2017: 87–8).
- The average age of a first-time buyer in the UK rose from 25 in 1969 to 30 in 2010 to 36 by 2014 (Lund, 2016: 116).
- According to the 2017 Housing White Paper, home ownership among 25–34 year olds in England has fallen from 59% just over a decade ago to 37%.
- Research suggests that in 2017, parents will have lent their children £6.5 billion to buy property, up from £5 billion in 2016, making the clichéd 'bank of mum and dad' the UK's ninth-biggest mortgage lender.[14]

The next chapter explores the nature of the housing crisis in more detail. It is encouraging that the government recognises the unfairness of ever-rising property prices. To quote the Housing White Paper:

> In 21st century Britain it's no longer unusual for houses to 'earn' more than the people living in them. In 2015, the average home in the South East of England increased in value by £29,000, while the average annual pay in the region was just £24,542. The average London home made its owner more than £22 an hour during the working week in 2015 – considerably more than the average Londoner's hourly rate. That's good news if you own a property in the capital, but it's a big barrier to entry if you don't. (DCLG, 2017a: 9)

However, Ministers are too keen to suggest a simple causal connection between housing supply and house prices (see Box 1.3). There clearly is a relationship between the two, but it is a long-term one. Countries with lax planning systems and frenetic house building, such as Ireland, Spain and the US, nevertheless experienced strong house price inflation before the global economic crash of 2008.

Box 1.3: A-level economics

You don't need a degree in economics to understand what happens when supply fails to keep up with demand. Across the country the average house now costs almost 8 times average earnings – an all-time record high. (Barwell, 2017)

The starting point is to build more homes. This will slow the rise in housing costs so that more ordinary working families can afford to buy a home and it will also bring the cost of renting down. (Theresa May, quoted in DCLG, 2017a: 5)

Soaring prices and rising rents caused by a shortage of the right homes in the right places has slammed the door of the housing market in the face of a whole generation. (Sajid Javid, quoted in DCLG, 2017a: 7)

> The laws of supply and demand mean the result is simple. Since 1998, the ratio of average house prices to average earnings has more than doubled. (DCLG, 2017a: 9)

There are many causes of house price and rent inflation in addition to undersupply. Economic growth, interest rates, the tax regime, the attractiveness of other investments and many other things play a part. At any given time, nine tenths of the houses on sale are second-hand, so a big increase in the supply of new homes has relatively little effect in the short term. It is worth noting that even Kate Barker's very thorough review of housing for Gordon Brown only aimed to bring down the rate of house price inflation, not to bring down house prices. The Barker review suggested that a near-doubling of output (to around 300,000 homes a year) would still leave house prices rising by 1.1% a year above inflation (CPRE, 2005: 22–5, 43–4).

There is a dishonesty in governments talking only about increased supply as a way to improve affordability while ignoring the many other tools at their disposal, and while they take policy decisions that will clearly stoke house price inflation.

- Lower- and middle-income house buyers are subsidised through schemes such as Help to Buy, even though this makes house prices even less affordable in the long run.
- For 50 years, homeowners have been supported in various ways through the tax system.
- Property taxes are remarkably inefficient, with no council tax revaluation or new bands introduced in England since the system was introduced in 1993.
- In the last 10 years, quantitative easing has injected some £1.2 trillion into the UK economy. This has pushed up the value of assets, widening the wealth gap between owners (who 'have made out like bandits' [Thompson, 2017]) and renters.
- High inheritance tax thresholds encourage people to invest in property, and entrench inequality.

- Rent controls are controversial, but other countries manage to protect tenants from exploitative landlords (Urban, 2015). While there is a shortage of supply, landlords will continue to bump up rents, which, in turn, feeds house price inflation.

So, while it really is scandalous that homes 'earn' more than their owners, it is mainly so because it is the result of deliberate policies pursued by successive governments. It is considered less electorally damaging to build houses on green fields and in the Green Belt than to tax housing wealth or curb house prices. The next section explores the complex relationship between land prices and house prices.

Land prices: who created the increment?

It is right to pin some of the blame for our failure to build enough houses on the planning system. However, where the system has been truly culpable is in its failure to control rising land prices. This is down to its weakness: what is needed is more planning, not less.

The 1947 settlement had two sides. It constrained development, aiming to preserve a clear physical distinction between town and country. This aspect of the system remains in place, however tattered. It is what planning is known for and why it is under attack in some quarters. But the system also ensured a plentiful supply of development land at reasonable prices. In particular, between 1946 and 1970, work started on 32 new towns, a programme that Nicholas Crane (2016: 497) describes as 'the single greatest exercise in systematic "town planting" since Alfred founded his *burhs* one thousand years earlier'.[15] The new towns are now home to 2.76 million people, 4.3% of UK households (Ryan-Collins et al, 2017: 81).

It was possible to create new towns because development corporations were given the power to buy land at agricultural value, using the uplift in value that came with planning permission to fund the development. Thus it was that land contributed only around 1% of the cost of a new home in Milton Keynes when it was first developed as a 'locally led' new town (it was proposed by Buckinghamshire County

Council as a way of stopping sporadic development across the county) (Ellis and Henderson, 2014: 128).

Land value capture was at the heart of wartime debates about post-war reconstruction. Pre-war, planning was toothless because the high cost of compensating landowners deterred local authorities from vetoing undesirable developments. But state intervention became more acceptable in the course of the war. If bombed areas of Britain were to be rebuilt and 'homes for heroes' provided, as they had not been after the Great War, it would be necessary to nationalise development rights and ensure that planning permission did not immediately inflate land prices.

That was the recommendation of Lord Uthwatt's committee on compensation and betterment, appointed in 1941. Churchill initially accepted it. In a broadcast on 26 March 1944, he said that there was 'a magnificent opportunity for rebuilding and replanning, and, while we are at it, we had better make a clean sweep of all those areas of which our civilisation should be ashamed'. He promised that 'ample land' would be made available 'at values fixed before war-time conditions supervened'. Local authorities would be able 'to secure any land required for the reconstruction of our towns and cities'. The value of the land would be 'between one-twentieth and one-thirtieth of the cost of the houses to be built upon it' (Churchill, 1945: 46–8).

Churchill's speech recalls a time when what was identified as a housing crisis prompted muscular action by the state. In the event, a backlash within the Conservative Party forced him to retreat. Difficult decisions on betterment were left to the Attlee government, and duly opposed by Churchill's Conservatives (though Churchill himself, bored by betterment, was busy writing his memoirs). However, it is worth reminding Conservatives that their greatest leader was, for a while at least, prepared to take on landowners and land speculators.

The justification for capturing land value is straightforward. The increased value of land that comes with development does not belong to the landowner because it results from the granting of planning permission, and the right to grant planning permission belongs (as all parties agree) to the state. The view that the lucky owner of agricultural or vacant land is the undeserving beneficiary of development pre-dates the planning system. The land question bulked large in Edwardian politics, particularly around the 1909 People's Budget. Lloyd George gave the example of marshland in London's Lea Valley:

> All that land became valuable building land, and land which used to be rented at £2 or £3 an acre has been selling within the last few years at £2,000 an acre, £3,000 an acre, £6,000 an acre, £8,000 an acre. Who created that increment? It was purely the combined efforts of all the people engaged in the trade and commerce of the Port of London – trader, merchant, ship-owner, dock labourer, workman, everyone except the landlord. (Speech in Limehouse, 30 July 1909, quoted in Lund, 2016: 36)

Similar arguments are made today about the disparity between the cost of agricultural land and land with planning permission. The conclusion often drawn is that land with planning permission costs a lot because it is scarce; freeing up planning would make more land available and therefore bring down its price. But land has a very important characteristic that those who want to release more in order to bring its price down neglect: it is finite. Wealth and aspiration, however, are ever-increasing. As wealth grows, the value of land will always go up even if the population remains stable. Land is a positional good for which there is, in the long term, insatiable demand. As wealth grows, people will want bigger homes, second homes, third homes, a pony paddock, a bigger pony paddock and so on. A weak planning system and plenty of available land will not stop land price or property bubbles. Even if 10 times more land was released for development, it would still carry a hefty premium. In a globalised world, this is a particular problem for global cities (see Box 1.4).

Box 1.4: Too much money chasing too little land: the problem of global cities

London attracts money from across the world and it is common for apartments in new developments to be marketed first to overseas investors. A 2017 report from Transparency International assessed 14 London developments worth at least £1.6 billion. It found that less than a quarter of the homes were bought by buyers based in the UK. Four out of 10 were sold through anonymous companies or to investors from countries with a high risk of corruption (Transparency International, 2017). Manchester also has a booming property market, and according to property journalist David Thame, investors are not pouring money into the city 'to provide cheaper space. It's to push house prices up as close as they can get to London prices. At which point, when it reaches its peak, they will move on somewhere else' (quoted in Williams, 2017). There is no necessary connection between increasing housing supply and meeting housing need; increased supply can benefit overseas investors and make life more difficult for local people.

Home ownership in the centre of all the world's most attractive cities is increasingly becoming the preserve of the global super-rich. New York's housing situation has been described as a 'humanitarian crisis'. According to Michael Greenberg (2017), writing in the *New York Review of Books*, three quarters of the city's homeless are families with children and at least a third of adults in these families have jobs: 'The bank teller, the maintenance worker, the delivery person, the nanny, the deli man, the security guard – any number of people we cross paths with every day – may be living, unbeknownst to us, in a shelter.'

Some cities are fighting to ensure that homes remain affordable. The Mayor of New York is giving tenants stronger protection against eviction. The Mayor of London has highlighted the issue of overseas ownership, though, at the time of writing, he seems unsure how to tackle it. Vancouver has a 15% tax on foreign owners buying property. Berlin, where renting is the norm, controls rents so that they cannot rise more than 10% above those for similar properties in the local area. Expensive redevelopments are banned in 33 districts, and in 2016, the city government blocked the sale of an apartment block to an offshore company (Minton, 2017: 122–3). Even so, the city seems to be on the brink of change, and the number of owner-occupied buildings is on the rise (Urban, 2015: 193).

It is not easy to control house prices in booming cities. It is certainly not possible to build one's way to a solution. It is delusional to think that simply releasing more land for development ('Build in the Green Belt!') will make housing in London affordable. Money will still pour in. This is not to argue against building more homes for a city's growing population. But where a city's property market has become, in Duncan Bowie's (2017: 68) words, 'a bank for surplus international wealth', regulation will have a bigger effect than house building. Indeed, without regulation, the newly built houses are likely to be snapped up by investors, compounding the problem of growing inequality.

It is important to assert the principle that whether land with planning permission costs 10 times or a thousand times more than land without, the landowner should not reap the uplift for doing nothing more than selling it. Some system of land value capture is imperative if we are to tackle the growing unaffordability of housing and build the homes we need. We cannot continue to go on as we are. I have already given the exceptional example of Milton Keynes, where agricultural land was assembled and compulsorily purchased by a powerful development corporation. More typically, land contributed less than 5% to housing costs in the 1930s, around 10% in the 1960s, 20% in the 1970s and 40% by the late 1990s (Lund, 2016: 33).

The development corporations that built the new towns largely paid for themselves because they were able to borrow cheaply, buy cheaply and then capture the land value uplift that they created through development (Ryan-Collins et al, 2017: 81). Today, land shoots up in price as soon as there is the prospect of planning permission. It is easier to agree the principle of capturing land value than it is to do it; there is a long history of failed attempts. But the fact that the 'property-owning democracy' is increasingly becoming a historical term should act as a powerful prompt, even for Conservatives traditionally protective of property rights.

What we have now is the worst of all worlds: land is too expensive and made more expensive by the fact that developers (private companies) have public obligations loaded on to them to fund affordable housing, roads and schools. I do not weep for the developers. Indeed, in the last few years, I have often wished I had shares in them. But the extra cost of the planning obligations is factored into the price of the land, which has two consequences.

First, it makes houses more expensive. Second, because the big national builders work on the basis of a 20% profit margin, they will, counter-intuitively, give a higher priority to developing where land prices are higher. When I visited King's Lynn with Sir Henry Bellingham, the local MP, I was struck by the fact that council planners had no confidence that the big house builders would develop all the sites for which they had permission. Any downturn or softening in demand and they would prioritise schemes in Cambridge or London: higher land prices, costlier planning obligations, but greater profits. As Ryan-Collins et al (2017: 96) put it: 'national house builders operate on a business model that focuses on controlling and trading land in high-demand areas, as this is … the source of the greatest profits'.

Land has not been a political issue in England for over a century, but housing is now so unaffordable and the environmental challenges we face so great that it should be. The New Economics Foundation's ground-breaking book *Rethinking the economics of land and housing* (Ryan-Collins et al, 2017), much quoted here, makes a compelling case for the importance of land to national wealth and well-being. Scotland has a Land Use Strategy and Wales is developing a National Development Framework. England needs to catch up and think about how to use land more strategically (CPRE, 2017a).

There is a growing willingness across parties to intervene in the shady land market through greater powers of compulsory purchase and 'use it or lose it' powers to ensure that planning permissions are used. This is difficult territory, both ideologically and operationally. However, it will not be possible to build the houses that the country needs without tackling the cost of land. This is a much more important issue than whether we build in the Green Belt. Under the current system, the price of Green Belt land would shoot up as soon as it was released. This would be good for investors and land speculators, but would do little for housing affordability.

One practical proposal for addressing inflated land costs is particularly worth considering. Currently, when a local authority buys land, it must pay a price that takes into account potential planning permission and investment in infrastructure. The Centre for Progressive Capitalism proposes a relatively simple reform to the Land Compensation Act 1961 that would enable local authorities to assemble and buy land at current use value, enabling them to invest an estimated £185 billion over the next 20 years in house building and infrastructure.[16]

There are other models available. As we leave the EU, perhaps we can start to learn from Europe. Peter Hall's last book, *Good cities, better lives: How Europe discovered the lost art of urbanism* (Hall, 2014), could have been titled 'They do things so much better abroad.' I am usually suspicious of the idea that one country does everything wrong while others do it all right. However, on the question of active local authorities with the power and vision to plan their growth, there is certainly much that we can learn. The story here is one of planning in the round: jobs, sustainable transport and green spaces, not just units of housing. Here are a few examples.

- In the Netherlands, 'the local authority plays a pivotal role in land assembly, often owning key sites, or enabling different ownerships to be pooled'. This makes it possible to find 'innovative ways of catering for previously-untapped markets' such as custom-built homes and various forms of co-housing (private homes with communal facilities). Hall sums up how it works: 'Effectively, a public corporation parcels out the land to private developers who competitively bid to build different residential areas – but all following neighbourhood master plans which in turn fit into the overall [national] concept' (Hall, 2014: 170–2). Long-term, low-cost loans from the municipal development bank encourage quality development. This is not the 'build and move on' model of most UK house builders: developers and local authorities are in it for the long haul.

  It is worth noting that Peter Hall's enthusiasm for ever-expanding towns and cities is questioned by Frank Wassenberg (2015: 219), who notes that the population of the Netherlands has grown steeply, and the number of households even faster, and that everyone wants more space: 'The only solution is to make better use of our existing cities, and limit new developments. This will protect the countryside as well.'

- Freiburg, in Germany, has two large urban extensions. From the start, planners worked closely with groups of citizens, jointly master planning the development. The city acquired the land before developments started and built the necessary (highly sustainable) infrastructure using investment funds through a trust. Sites were then sold to builders and individuals. 'This has worked triumphantly', says Hall (2014: 258), 'because good location and brilliant design have generated huge demand, effectively allowing the process to self-fund itself.'

- A final example, not from Peter Hall's book, is Hamburg's ambitious plan to cover over two miles of the autobahn that runs through the city. The scheme will create 60 acres of new green space, and also space for 2,000 new homes.[17] It would be good to see similarly bold schemes of this sort in the UK.

We turn now to the reason why it is so important to build new homes.

Notes

[1] See: www.conservativemanifesto.com/1951/1951-conservative-manifesto.shtml

[2] Department for Communities and Local Government (DCLG), Live tables on house building, Table 244. Available at: https://www.gov.uk/government/statistical-data-sets/live-tables-on-house-building

[3] See also Martin Crookston's (2014: 166) warning against 'letting the market do your social engineering for you'.

[4] https://order-order.com/2016/01/19/osbornes-chopper-donor-benefits-from-planning-reforms/

[5] See: www.channel4.com/info/press/news/secrets-of-britain-s-new-homes-channel-4-dispatches

[6] See: www.leaseholdknowledge.com/bloor-homes-builds-leasehold-houses-gives-400000-conservative-party

[7] See: www.bournemouthecho.co.uk/news/13320237.650_house_development_on_former_greenbelt_will_be__new_town___warn_campaigners/

[8] Policy Exchange has not entirely abandoned its hostility to planning. Its August 2017 report 'Farming tomorrow: British agriculture after Brexit' (Policy Exchange, 2017) proposes withdrawing agricultural subsidies and building houses on 'marginal' farming land.

[9] See: www.bbc.co.uk/news/business-36501536. In April 2017, the *Daily Mail* reported that Persimmon's chief executive was set to receive a bonus worth £112 million, see: www.dailymail.co.uk/news/article-4453992/Housing-boss-profited-leaseholds-gets-112m-bonus.html. *The Guardian* reported that the chief executive's bonus could be used to build 1,375 council houses, see: www.theguardian.com/business/2017/dec/30/a-fraction-of-persimmon-bosss-110m-bonus-could-house-all-homeless-of-york.

[10] Of her education, she says: 'survive five years in a school on a council estate and you get a medal from the Nietzsche Society' (Hanley, 2007: 155).

[11] The percentage of public expenditure devoted to house building fell from 5.6% in 1981 to just 1% in the year 2000. *The blunders of our governments* by Anthony King and Ivor Crewe (2013) seeks to explain why 'today's British governments screw up so often'.

[12] See: www.huffingtonpost.co.uk/dan-wilson-craw/register-to-vote_b_16624616.html

[13] See: www.savills.co.uk/_news/article/72418/213407-0/1/2017/uk-homes-worth-a-record-%C2%A36.8-trillion-as-private-housing-wealth-exceeds-%C2%A35-trillion

[14] See: https://www.cebr.com/reports/the-bank-of-mum-and-dad-in-2017-will-help-buy-homes-worth-over-75bn-and-fund-more-than-one-in-four-property-transactions-in-the-uk/. It is worth noting that Legal and General, who sponsored the research, have a strong financial interest in house building.

[15] Crane is referring specifically to the 14 new towns designated between 1946 and 1950.

[16] See: http://progressive-capitalism.net/2017/10/market-prices-housing-crisis/

[17] See 'They're going to bury a stretch of German autobahn and cover it in parks.' Available at: https://www.fastcompany.com/3040310/theyre-going-to-bury-a-stretch-of-german-autobahn-and-cover-it-in-parks

TWO

The housing crisis

Most of us dislike the ugliness of much of the building development now proceeding, but we must realise and sympathise with the fact that people are no longer content to live in crowded, and sometimes dingy, streets in the towns, and that new houses in the country, and particularly within reach of the towns, are inevitable. The countryside can absorb a vast number of new houses without serious injury if suitably grouped and sited and built of pleasant materials which blend with their surroundings. (Foreword by the Rt Hon The Earl of Derby KG to *Building in Lancashire* [CPRE Lancashire, 1937], quoted in Crookston, 2016: 7)

Even while battling inappropriate new housing, conservationists should remember that we really do need to build many more houses. This will entail some loss of countryside, though how 'vast' a number of new homes the countryside can absorb is open to question. The exact nature of the housing crisis, however, needs unpacking, as do the solutions. Crude claims that we must build over lots of countryside in order to achieve 230,000, 250,000, 300,000 or more homes a year are misguided and, because they get people's backs up, counterproductive.

We have a shortage of particular types of homes for particular people in particular places. Simply building lots more homes across the country will not, in itself, address the problem, which is partly one of growing inequality between north and south, young and old, and those with a chance of getting on the 'property ladder' and those with no chance. It matters where the new homes are built and how they are shared out. More five-bedroom villas in the Green Belt, which is often what is on offer, will solve some problems (how to ensure bigger houses for wealthy people who want to live in the Green Belt; how to provide a new investment vehicle for those with excess cash) but will not provide what is needed: a decent home for everyone at a price they can afford.

The chapter starts by considering whether it would be easier to tackle the housing challenge if we stopped immigration and lived shorter, less fecund lives. This is a question often avoided in liberal society, but half the online comments under any newspaper article on housing call for population controls.

Population

Population growth is a major driver of housing demand. After a long period of stability, net immigration added around 4 million people to the UK's population in the space of just 15 years. According to the anti-immigration campaign Migration Watch, 'we will need to build one home every four minutes for the next 25 years just to house future migrants and their children'.[1] This is a contestable statement, but one gets the point. When I spoke at the annual general meeting (AGM) of the Dorset branch of the Campaign to Protect Rural England (CPRE) in November 2016 on 'the urbanisation of Dorset', I recalled an Office for National Statistics (ONS) estimate that the UK's population is set to grow by 440,000 people a year, more than the county's current population.[2] No wonder the branch is worried about urbanisation.

David Attenborough says that 'all our environmental problems become easier to solve with fewer people, and harder – and ultimately impossible – to solve with ever more people'.[3] Population is an environmental issue and England's growing population has an immediate impact on CPRE's main concern, the sustainable use of land and other finite natural resources. So, should we have spoken out when New Labour embarked on policies that would result in what David Goodhart has called a 'demographic revolution', Britain's 'largest wave of immigration ever'?[4]

Some clearly thought so. In my time with CPRE, I received more letters on this issue than any other. However, I never felt that anything CPRE did would alter the UK's population by a single person. Successive governments have been committed to reducing immigration, so there was no political argument to win even if we had wanted to. But they have failed to do so because although immigration may be unpopular, the things it brings with it (economic growth; tax income; people to pick our crops, serve our drinks and tend to us in hospital; partners and friends) are not.

Even if we immediately stopped all immigration, over half the projected growth in population is already 'in the system', owing to increased birth rates and longevity. Those who will form households in the next 20 years are already born. The uncertainty is over migration, which rests partly on policy and partly on the state of the economy (Beckett, 2016). An economic crash will reduce immigration, and may come with Brexit, but it is hardly desirable. I would rather live in a country people want to come to than one they want to leave.

Population numbers are important, but so are patterns of consumption. Higher housing densities and better use of land can save a good deal of countryside even as we build houses. A country of 70 or 80 million people with the right policies and culture can live more sustainably than a country of 30 or 40 million with the wrong ones.

CPRE's main concern is how people live, not how many people are doing the living, and my main concern as chief executive was that talking about population at every turn, as many urged, would dilute our message and undermine our influence. I wish, though, that I had thought more about the issue when New Labour was (without quite knowing what it was doing) taking decisions that would massively increase the population. This was environmentally significant, and the green lobby was largely silent. I acknowledge that a degree of liberal distaste for the anti-immigration lobby influenced my stance.

However, CPRE did not ignore the issue. We debated it many times at board level, in our policy committee and at AGMs. Perhaps we should have said loudly and clearly: 'if you pursue this policy, we will need more houses, more energy, more food, etc'. But I am not convinced that anyone would have taken any notice, and in any case, these are not clinching arguments. It would be perfectly in order to weigh the environmental impact of immigration and still support it for economic reasons or out of a desire to be an open, diverse country. Once you accept a degree of population growth as a given, the environmental argument is about how to accommodate it, and that is where CPRE has put its effort.

The Barker review

In March 2004, Kate Barker's review of housing supply called for a step change in the supply of market housing to bring down the rate of house price inflation, as well as an additional 17,000–23,000 social homes a year to improve access for those who cannot afford market housing. The lower figure would keep up with demographic trends, while the higher figure would address the backlog of need. The report also called for 'a more flexible housing market, one in which supply responds more strongly to changes in price' (Barker, 2004: 5). In other words, house prices should become a major influence in planning and more land should be released for development to prevent them rising too sharply.

Kate Barker's brief was to look at 'issues underlying the lack of supply and responsiveness of housing in the UK', including the role of the planning system (Barker, 2004: 3). Bafflingly, she was not asked to consider demand-side factors that have led people to put their money in property, such as low interest rates, favourable taxation, easy credit and the relatively poor performance of other investments. Her remit simply assumed that the problem was a lack of supply.

The Barker review posited a relatively straightforward relationship between supply and house prices: if 70,000 more private sector homes were built each year compared with 2002/03, prices would be 1.8% higher than inflation and more or less in line with the growth in real earnings; if 120,000 more were built, the trend rate of house price inflation would reduce to 1.1%. Well, maybe. But what about all the other variables that affect house prices?

CPRE (2005) published a formidable critique of the Barker thesis, *Building on Barker*, but within a few years, we had accepted that there was, indeed, a chronic undersupply of housing and that the country needed to build many more houses. Much of Kate Barker's thesis, which quietly influences the current government, still seems flawed, but the need to speed up the rate at which we build became increasingly evident even before the 2008 economic crash hit house building.

Three of CPRE's principal reasons for rejecting the idea of a chronic undersupply ceased to hold within a few years of the review's publication (CPRE, 2005: 20–2). First, we argued that owner occupation had increased from 67% to 71% of households between 1993 and 2003, and was still increasing. However, 2003 turned out to be its peak year. By 2015/16, it had declined to 63% of households (DCLG, 2017b). Second, we argued that house prices had risen no faster than average earnings over the previous decade. This is no longer the case. Third, when the Barker report was issued, household size in England had been falling for 90 years. It was 2.67 people per household in 1981, 2.47 in 1991 and 2.36 in 2001. 'If there was a serious long term shortage of housing', we said, 'it would have halted or curtailed this trend' (CPRE, 2005: 20). This is precisely what happened. The average household size in England in 2011 was still 2.36 people (ONS, 2014: 15).

CPRE increasingly came to accept the concept of a 'housing crisis'. Far too many people live in housing conditions that shame our rich nation or pay ludicrous sums of money for inadequate and insecure housing, and the situation is getting worse. We joined the calls of pretty well everyone else for more house building. However, to accept that there is a housing crisis does not mean abandoning one's critical faculties.

Crisis, what crisis?

We should retain a degree of scepticism about household projections. They are necessary for planning but unreliable and hard to interpret. The 2011 census surprised demographers. It showed that there were 450,000 more people in England than in the ONS's 2010-based population projections, but 290,000 fewer households than in the Department for Communities and Local Government's (DCLG's) 2008-based population projections (McDonald and Williams, 2014: 3). If ever you need a snapshot of the hazards of planning for housing on the basis of projections, there it is. The consensus view is that fewer households were formed because young adults could not afford the homes that would enable them to form households. That reinforces the 'crisis' frame, but it is a retrospective judgement. Projections need to be treated with care.

We should also remember that the number of new homes built is less important than net additions to the housing stock. Almost all the debate is on the number of new homes built. The last year in which more than 200,000 were completed in England was 1988/89: 202,930 dwellings, at the height of the Lawson boom.[5] What is often forgotten is that when the country was building over 300,000 homes a year, it was also clearing slums. Between 1961 and 1973/74, there were at least 60,000 demolitions each year, with a peak of 74,700 in 1971 (Holmans, 2005: 58).[6] Before 1980, the net increase in housing stock was generally lower than the number of homes built; since 1980, with fewer slums demolished and more buildings converted for residential use, new additions have generally exceeded the number of new homes built (House of Commons Library, 2017).

If you look at net additions to the housing stock (DCLG, 2016a) rather than new-build, the delivery of new homes does not look quite so bad, at least in the good years. In the 13 years from 1991/92 to 2003/04, there were just over 2 million net additions to the housing stock in England, an average of 154,000 extra dwellings a year. It was in March 2004 that the Barker review was published: 'I do not believe that continuing at the current rate of housebuilding is a realistic option', Kate Barker (2004: 1) said.

In the 12 years following the Barker review, there was an average of 171,000 net additions, in spite of the impact of the 2008 economic crash. In each of the three years leading up to the crash, there were over 200,000 net additions, peaking at 223,530 in 2007/08. Net additions dropped to 124,720 in 2012/13, the lowest for decades, but picked up to just over 170,000 in 2014/15 and almost 190,000 in 2015/16. Depending on your point of view, this suggests either that the planning system was delivering or that the private sector builds (and converts buildings) when the economy is strong and fails to do so when it is weak, whatever the system.

The latest household projections suggest that we need to increase the supply of new housing (DCLG, 2016b). The number of households in England is projected to increase from 22.7 million in 2014 to 28 million in 2039, an annual growth of 210,000 households a year. Average household size is (once again) projected to fall, from 2.35 in 2014 to 2.21 in 2039. Households headed by those aged 65 or over (the generation with property wealth) are set to increase by 155,000 a year; those headed by 25 to 34 year olds are set to decrease by 9,000 per year, not because of a slowing of population growth, but because people in this age cohort will take longer to form households. One-person households are projected to grow by 68,000 a year. The projections suggest a need for smaller properties, including homes specifically for older people.

There is a judgement to be made about how easily one should be able to form a household. Property has never been limitless, but most people would surely accept that there is something seriously wrong with a housing system that forces couples in their 30s with children to live with their parents. The country has become richer, but the patterns of occupation that my generation took to be normal have been denied to the next generation.

That is why I am uncomfortable with the argument of Ian Mulheirn of Oxford Economics that because households are not forming as they once did, there is no need to increase output.[7] Official projections, he says, have consistently overestimated the number of households for whom homes must be provided. In 2008, the DCLG forecast that about 280,000 households would form each year up to 2016; the 2014 projections suggested 235,000 a year. Mulheirn says:

> In light of those expectations it's easy to see why you might worry about undersupply when the housing stock is growing at under 200k per year. But the reality – or, at least, the best evidence we have – is that the number of UK households has been growing at only 152k per year since 2008. Consequently we now appear to have a whopping 1.2 million fewer households in the country than was anticipated in 2008. Even if we want to err on the side of caution, it's hard to see how the UK needs more than 200k per year to keep pace with household growth at present.

This is a good reason for scepticism, for interrogating the figures and questioning *ex cathedra* pronouncements that we need to build x-thousand new homes a year. Projections are not predictions. The government's household projections vary hugely from exercise to exercise and, as Muheirn says, generally bear very little relationship to what actually transpires. Brexit adds further uncertainty: we do not know what will happen to immigration (which accounts for 37% of projected household growth), or economic growth, or, come to that, emigration if people start leaving the country.

However, we should be worried about the phenomenon of suppressed households and young people finding it hard to find a decent place to live. Furthermore, we should worry about the contribution of unevenly shared property wealth to growing inequality in our country. Building more homes is not the solution to these problems, but it is *part* of the solution.

The perils of target-based policy

So, how many homes do we need to build? Some high numbers are
thrown out. For example, a 2016 House of Lords Economic Affairs
Select Committee (2016: 4) report asserted that 'at least 300,000 homes
a year need to be built for the foreseeable future' in order to meet
future demand, make up for a backlog of undersupply and moderate
house prices. The report is widely cited, but the figure of 300,000 is
backed by precious little evidence: it is just confident, lordly assertion.

Does it matter? I think it does because obsessing about the numbers
distracts from the equally important question of how property is
distributed: who owns what and where, as well as how it is shared
out. It draws attention from taxation, regulation and other means of
controlling house prices and rents. It sets a frame that immediately
encourages one to think in terms of a lack of supply as the reason for
homelessness, high rents, unaffordable mortgages and so on. It also
guarantees disappointment as neither the private nor public sector has
the capacity or ambition to build on this scale.

Without a radical shift in policy, significant public money and the
sort of investment in skills and new providers that will take years
to bear fruit, there is no chance of output reaching and staying at
300,000 homes a year. To achieve anything like that number would
require governments to give the highest priority to housing, which
seems highly unlikely as they deal with the fallout from Brexit. They
would have to stop mucking around with planning and housing policy
every couple of years, and appoint senior ministers within the cabinet
to champion house building. With a single-minded determination
that has eluded governments in recent years, and the sort of policies
proposed in the final chapter, we can build more houses. However,
those pushing for high numbers also need to consider how to achieve
this increased output without further reducing the quality of design
and place making.

As things stands, grand statements that we need to build 250,000
or 300,000 homes every year are bluster, designed to signal virtue or
prod the national debate in support of house building. The trouble

is that when unachievable targets guide planning policy, they result in unnecessary loss of countryside and poor-quality development. We should build in ways that benefit society and do the least possible damage to the environment. That may seem a statement of the obvious, but, in recent years, targets have become ends in themselves, not a means of creating better places and improving lives. Increased supply is not a panacea for our housing ills. At least 200,000 net additions to the housing stock each year seems a reasonable aspiration, but our first priority should be a decent home for everyone at a price they can afford, not meeting aspirational demand (see Chapter Five).

Location, location

It is often said that we need to build where people want to live. The line is repeated by politicians, commentators and economists, and it sounds right. Who would argue for building homes where no one wants to live?

But predict-and-provide policies become self-reinforcing. We build homes where there are jobs and then create more jobs for the people drawn to the area; increased investment in transport and services attracts yet more jobs and more people to do them; more houses are built, and even more needed. So it goes on. Meanwhile, other towns and cities are starved of the money and attention that might attract people to them.

We should contest the assumption that the future must be like the recent past and that the job of planning is to respond to and reinforce market trends. There is no inevitability. Public policy can shape markets and alter how and where people want to live. London is buzzing now, but when I first got to know it in the late 1970s, it was a grey place that people wanted to leave. The same applies to Manchester, Liverpool, Birmingham and Sheffield, all of which seemed to be in inexorable decline 30 or 40 years ago. Partly because of rising prosperity, but also because Green Belts and brownfield-first policies concentrated investment within the cities, their decline was reversed. Or consider Milton Keynes and other new towns. People did not clamour to move to them when they were first built; there was a strategy for making them places people wanted to live.

There is a serious flaw in today's efforts to rebalance economic growth. I do not doubt politicians' commitment to the 'Northern Powerhouse', the 'Midlands Engine' and so on, but they have no chance of success while disproportionate investment is poured into London and the South-East. We are told that nothing must endanger the prosperity of 'UK plc', but UK plc does not exist: it is a category error. The UK is not a plc and, as has been endlessly discussed since Brexit, the places left behind in the rush for economic growth (those places 'just about managing') may actively resent those that are doing well.

It is depressing when clichés shape thinking, but the UK plc mindset is not new. I recall a CPRE seminar on rebalancing growth under the last Labour government. A minister representing a northern constituency simply could not process the idea that if an overseas company offered to create 200 jobs in a part of Surrey with full employment, a housing shortage and lots of Green Belt, it would be sensible (at the very least) to encourage it to invest elsewhere. The assumption was that UK plc needed the jobs (even if Surrey did not) and that there was no point in trying to redirect investment. I discussed a similar dilemma with an MP whose constituency lies mostly within a National Park. A small manufacturer there won a big contract necessitating significant expansion. The new jobs were low-paid and would be filled by incomers to the area, mostly from overseas. However, no one was prepared to say 'put them in Stoke'. The result was more housing pressure in a pressured, expensive rural town and no new jobs in Stoke (or Burnley or Rochdale or any of the places that most need them).

Ministers are now keen to show that Brexit Britain is 'open for business', which means more roads in the South-East (notably, the Lower Thames Crossing, designed both to ease congestion *and* generate jobs and housing: 'go figure'[8]), new ports (a deep-water port at Dibden Bay in the New Forest is being talked up by ministers to draw more jobs to booming Hampshire) and, most significantly, the third runway at Heathrow.

A Treasury civil servant told me that the new runway will 'unlock' 80,000 jobs. What he meant was that many more people will have to be accommodated in an area that already has a housing shortage. Heathrow is set to become the biggest airport in the world, sucking yet more money and employment to the richest part of the country, and one of the most environmentally pressured. Some of this was considered by the Airports Commission, which recommended the new runway, but its report suggests that growth always comes first and that housing pressures and spatial inequality are afterthoughts (Airports Commission, 2015). Paragraph 6.27 promises that it will explain 'how any additional demand for new housing might be accommodated through increasing density and expansion in workforce catchment areas', but you will search the report in vain for any such explanation.

It is hard to escape the conclusion that neither the Airports Commission nor the government that accepted its recommendation thought very hard about the land-use implications of creating thousands more jobs in an area with housing stress and almost full employment. The Airports Commission (2015: para 6.90) argues that expanding either Heathrow or Gatwick would fit well with existing spatial plans, but that is because England, unlike most developed countries, lacks any sort of national spatial plan. It is time that we had one to help us make decisions of this sort that have consequences for the whole nation. The alternative is to carry on privileging already-privileged areas over those that are struggling (though privilege in the overheated South-East comes at a price).

Of course, there is no easy way to even out wealth. In a global world, it would be foolish to assume that jobs intended for London, Surrey or Oxford can simply be redirected to less thriving parts of the UK; they could equally go abroad or not be created at all. Furthermore, it is undeniable that a good deal of money has been spent on regeneration over decades, often with little to show for it. Some of the distressed areas of the 1930s continued to receive special assistance under the Blair government and remain distressed today.

As Chancellor, Geoffrey Howe thought that trying to regenerate Liverpool was like 'pumping water uphill'; 'managed decline' was preferable (Lund, 2016: 77). Almost 30 years later, Policy Exchange argued for abandoning northern cities that were in the 'wrong place' to thrive in the modern world: 'It is time to stop pretending that there is a bright future for Sunderland and ask ourselves instead what we need to do to offer people in Sunderland better prospects' (Leunig and Swafield, 2008: 62). The report argued that they should be encouraged to move south and that economically dynamic cities such as London, Oxford and Cambridge should be allowed to spread into the surrounding countryside (Leunig and Swaffield, 2008: 31).[9] David Cameron, so often influenced by Policy Exchange reports, branded this one 'insane'.

Pushing more development south will have environmental consequences. Parts of the South-East and East of England are at the limits of their environmental capacity: overdevelopment will mean more droughts, floods and air pollution. It will reduce people's ability to enjoy nature and the countryside close to where they live. There is also a moral dimension to the idea that we should abandon struggling parts of the country. Not everyone in a city like Sunderland wants to move south and, as Ellis and Henderson (2014: 42–3) write, it 'cannot be fair to write off people and communities, condemning them to a futureless existence'. Regeneration is hard work but it has not been a total failure: British cities have avoided the worst of the US experience. It may be true that our housing stock is not located where it is currently most needed, but that is not a conclusive argument for abandoning it. That would be a huge waste of land, carbon and potential.

Instead, we should get serious about rebalancing the country's economy. To quote Kate Barker (2014: 10) (a sceptic), tilting the economic geography of the UK from south to north will require 'improved skills and transport links, the movement of government offices out of London and the creation of new cultural centres'. This will not come easy to UK policymakers given the long-established centralism of the British state, London's extraordinary dominance over many centuries[10] and the laissez-faire approach of successive British governments. However, it is important to try. Our dysfunctional housing system results from spatial inequality, as well as inequality between individuals. We can weaken planning and watch these inequalities grow. We can plan to make them worse by pouring money into the South-East and starving the North of investment.[11] Or, we can reject either of these options and plan to reduce spatial inequality by using land more wisely and spreading wealth more fairly across the country.

The human cost of inadequate housing

Having addressed those who elevate output above all other considerations, and made a case for not overheating overheated parts of the country any more, I want to remind countryside campaigners that people pay a high cost for our failure to build enough of the right sort of homes. Poor housing blights lives. Conservationists get angry about the destruction, erosion and uglification of the countryside – rightly so. However, we should spare some anger for those suffering the consequences of the mess that the country has made of housing.

The high cost of home ownership means that the sort of people who would have been buying their first home a generation ago are now stuck in insecure, rented accommodation. They may have a good income but they lack wealth. According to the Institute for Fiscal Studies, the average household wealth of those in their early 30s is £27,000; those born in the 1970s had almost double this (£53,000) at the same age (Ryan-Collins et al, 2017: 182).

Go down the income scale and things get much worse. In February 2017, Shelter reported that 1.6 million families with children were living in private rented housing, with precious few rights. Tenancies run from one to 12 months, some on a rolling month-by-month basis, and the prospect of eviction can put tenants' lives on hold. The laws on private renting were written when it was assumed that this sort of accommodation was used mostly by people who only needed temporary housing, such as students and 20-somethings. Now, more and more families on low and middle incomes are renting. They cannot afford to buy and they have no chance of getting social housing. So, one in four families with children now rents from a private landlord, up from less than one in 10 in 2003. The number of children growing up in private rented accommodation more than doubled between the 2001 and 2011 censuses.

Over a quarter of renting parents have moved three times or more in the last five years. Such upheaval can have a terrible impact on a child's education and sense of security. Tenants need more security, and that can be delivered regardless of how many new homes are built. However, they also need more options, and that means building more homes. It also means that we must share wealth more equally so that older and better-off people are not so easily able to buy second and third homes to rent out, while families on decent wages despair of ever buying (Shelter, 2017a).

The prospects for private renters are perhaps not helped by the fact that so many MPs are private landlords. In the 2010 Parliament, 193 MPs, almost a third, were landlords.[12] The figure has fallen to 123, but this is partly because so many first-time MPs were elected in 2017.[13] In 2016, 72 landlord MPs voted against an amendment to the Housing and Planning Bill calling for all homes to be 'fit for human habitation'.[14] Some rental housing in all sectors is in a shocking condition and tenants have little protection. The impact on children is particularly harmful. The immediate answer is to improve the stock and protect tenants' rights, but people live in substandard homes because there are so few options. Part of the answer is to build more.

The last stop in this brief misery tour of poor housing concerns those in temporary accommodation. The Institute for Public Policy Research (IPPR) think tank collected stories from some of the 'hidden homeless' single people who end up in poor-quality bed-and-breakfast accommodation, private hostels and short-stay shared houses. The following is one extract:

It is a dump.... The quilt is just covered, soaked in blood. You have never seen anything like it. No heating. One person says [the landlord] has done nothing to maintain the place in 10 years. It is just so disgusting. I have been there just 24 hours and I am sleeping in all my clothes, my coat. Wrapped up and not touching anything. I have a scarf over my mouth so I don't breathe any disease in. (Davies, 2016)

Families too are increasingly housed in bed–and–breakfast accommodation. At the end of June 2015, almost 100,000 children were homeless and living in temporary accommodation, 80% of them in London. According to a *Guardian* report, one in 25 children in London, at least one for every classroom, lives in temporary accommodation.[15]

All this is shocking stuff. It does not argue for building villas in the Green Belt or more luxury flats on the Thames. Mere numbers of new homes are beside the point. Addressing these problems (one could add the growing scandal of rough sleeping) requires targeted public investment and stronger regulation. To suggest that all that is needed is more house building is to miss the point: it is like arguing that better-stocked supermarkets will obviate the need for food banks. However, part of the solution must be to address the chronic undersupply of new homes. This is a moral imperative, for conservationists as much as for anyone else.

Notes

[1] See: www.migrationwatchuk.org/key-topics/housing
[2] See: www.theguardian.com/world/2015/oct/29/uk-population-expected-to-rise-by-almost-10-million-in-25-years
[3] See: www.populationmatters.org/happy-90th-birthday-sir-david-attenborough/
[4] See: http://news.bbc.co.uk/1/hi/8494275.stm
[5] DCLG live tables on house building, Table 209, available at: www.gov.uk/government/statistical-data-sets/live-tables-on-house-building. Not only was the 1980s' building boom unsustainable, it also resulted in some pretty awful developments that 'smothered local identity, substituted low-density sprawl for clustered village communities and turned everything it touched into a suburb' (McGhie and Girling, 1996: 8).
[6] The statistics appear to be for Great Britain.

[7] See 'Is there really a housing shortage?', January 2017, available at: https://medium.com/@ian.mulheirn/part-1-is-there-really-a-housing-shortage-89fdc6bac4d2

[8] Highways England justifies the new tunnel on the grounds that it will 'unlock billions of pounds worth of economic benefit and create thousands of jobs. It opens opportunities for investment, for much needed housing and for businesses to grow. This will connect communities and improve access to jobs, housing, leisure and retail facilities either side of the river' (see: https://cpreviewpoint.wordpress.com/2017/04/28/on-the-marshes/). This is the growth paradigm in a couple of computer-generated sentences.

[9] As of October 2017, the co-author of the report, Tim Leunig, is senior policy adviser to the environment secretary and economic adviser to the communities secretary on housing supply.

[10] In 120 AD, London's (or Londinium's) population was 'far in excess of any other settlement in Britain'. By 1300, 'London was already a nation apart'. In 1600, its population was 13 times that of Norwich, the next largest city in Britain (Crane, 2016: 217, 322, 354).

[11] According to an Institute for Public Policy Research (IPPR) report in February 2017, the government spends £1,500 more per head on transport in London than in the North, see: https://www.ippr.org/news-and-media/press-releases/new-transport-figures-reveal-london-gets-1-500-per-head-more-than-the-north-but-north-west-powerhouse-catching-up

[12] See: https://www.theguardian.com/housing-network/2016/jan/14/mp-landlords-number-risen-quarter-last-parliament-housing-bill

[13] See: https://www.channel4.com/news/factcheck/almost-one-in-five-mps-are-landlords

[14] See: https://fullfact.org/economy/did-mps-vote-against-homes-having-be-made-fit-live-in/

[15] See: https://www.theguardian.com/housing-network/2015/nov/11/children-poor-housing-temporary-accommodation-health-education

THREE

Rural housing

The rural difference

The countryside is different. There are differences everywhere, of course, so we need place-specific approaches to house building. But in our urban society, the rural difference is particularly often overlooked.

Most villages are desirable places to live and, partly as a result, unaffordable to local people. Wages in rural areas tend to be around £5,000 a year lower than in urban areas, and there is less affordable housing: only 8% of rural homes are classified as affordable, compared with 20% in urban areas. Property prices are also higher. Developers swarm round villages with planning applications for executive homes, but there is a serious shortage of non-market housing. The Campaign to Protect Rural England's (CPRE's) 2015 report, *A Living Countryside* (Burroughs, 2015b: 12), showed that, in every region, average house prices were higher in rural than in urban areas. In the West Midlands, where the gap was greatest, the average rural home cost £244,000, compared with £155,000 for an urban home (Burroughs, 2015b: 12). In many villages, no amount of building will make market housing affordable to local people – that horse bolted long ago.

'The living tapestry of a mixed community'

Does this matter? Should we worry if villages are dominated by retirees and the better off, with the less well off driving in from towns to work or visit their relatives? After all, the death of the village has long been mourned, yet villages survive. 'The last days of my childhood were also the last days of the village', Laurie Lee wrote in *Cider with Rosie* (quoted in Rowley, 2006: 11). In *The country and the city*, Raymond Williams (1993: 9) recalled a book which claimed that 'A way of life that has come down to us from the days of Virgil has suddenly ended'; this, he thought, 'was curious. From Virgil? Here? A way of country life?'

Williams shows how writers in every generation, back at least to the Middle Ages, have declared rural England to be dead or dying (Williams, 1993: 9–12). However, the life that these writers lamented was hard for most people. If they loved the land, it was, as Richard Benson (2006: 35) puts it in his memoir *The farm*, 'only with the kind of love people had for the unforgiving Old Testament God who had cursed them with work, and who gave them their daily bread in the sweat of their faces, with no alternative'. In Britain, as in all countries, when rural people have had the chance to move into towns to enjoy a better, more exciting life, they have tended to do so.

This was particularly so from the last quarter of the 19th century, years of agricultural depression in much of the country. Trevor Rowley (2006: 218) records that many 'villages which lay further than ten miles or so from a major town or city were in decline until the 1960s, and rural depopulation was a major problem, as people left villages and services closed'. However, in the last 50 years, the trend has been the other way: 'Commuters, the retired and second home owners have returned to the village in large numbers' (Rowley, 2006: 218). They have come in search of a better quality of life and, perhaps, the rural idyll. In many cases, the physical fabric of the village has improved, but the social and age mix of the village has narrowed.

One cannot stop people wanting to move to the country, but if everyone who wants and is able to move does so, it will profoundly damage both the countryside and the towns and cities that they abandon. Rural landscapes will be eroded by housing and roads, and cities will lose wealth and social diversity. It is partly to avoid these outcomes that we have a town and country planning system. What Peter Hall called 'the containment of urban England' is necessary because there is almost no limit to the demand for market housing in most villages; it can only be met with damaging social and environmental consequences, ultimately at the price of destroying the village as a village.

Hall also argued that urban containment systematically excluded poorer people from rural areas, that countryside protection was a pretext for social exclusivity: keeping out the oiks. This is a charge frequently made against CPRE and its founders. In *On the marshes*, Carol Donaldson (2017a) recalls Patrick Abercrombie's distaste for the unplanned, self-built interwar settlements known as plotlands: 'The preserver of rural amenities cannot allow any sort of old junk cabin to deform the choicest spot', he said. Donaldson acknowledges that he had a point: 'If unchecked, many of our beauty spots would have been turned into a giant suburb. But', she says, 'beneath the desire to protect the countryside, there appears to have been an equal desire to protect it from the "wrong sort"' (Donaldson, 2017a: 38).

If this was once true of CPRE, I do not think it is now. You would expect CPRE to question and often oppose development in the countryside, but it is much more likely to support affordable than market housing. When we helped draw up the Rural Coalition's 2010 policy statement, *The rural challenge*,[1] I was concerned that some branches might object to its pro-development stance and strong support for permanently affordable housing. In the event, I received only one complaint: a branch chair who was also an active member of the Conservative Party objected to the recommendation that local authorities be allowed to retain all the income from selling council homes; we should, he said, have gone further and called for a total end to council house sales in rural areas.

Many country people think that the Right to Buy was a disaster for rural areas, which lost council housing at a faster rate than urban areas because most rural council properties were houses, not flats, and particularly attractive for home ownership. What was lacking was 'rural-proofing': a conscious effort to consider the rural dimension in policymaking. In recent years, national housing policy has seemed almost designed to intensify the shortage of affordable homes in rural areas. The fact is that if a village loses what little affordable housing it has, it will find it very hard to replace. There is a shortage of specialist providers, suitable land and money. Rural areas will become, even more than they are now, the preserve of the better off, which, in our society, tends to mean older people who already own property.

"They call it affordable housing, but I prefer to think of it as local homes for local people." (Participant at CPRE Kent focus group, April 2017)

Back to the question of whether this matters. A senior Tory adviser told me that no one has any more right to live in a village than someone brought up in Mayfair has a right to live there: if you cannot afford to live in your family's village, then that is tough. However, housing policy should be about more than mere bricks and mortar. It should aim for the 'living tapestry of a mixed community'. We associate this particularly with village life, but I also think we should provide affordable housing in or near property hot spots like Mayfair. The social cleansing of parts of London is as damaging in its own way, not only to the individuals 'cleansed', but also to the character of London, as the lifelessness of some picture-postcard Cotswold villages.

Besides, this is not just about letting people stay in the village of their birth. Jobs in villages are often poorly paid, and the lettings policies for new rural housing can reflect this. On the Stourhead Estate, Wiltshire, for instance, the lettings policy for four new affordable homes gives priority to those working in the village of Stourton.[2] Policies of this sort may, in time, even increase the ethnic diversity of villages. If they are to keep their social mix, villages need social housing, homes that will be affordable in perpetuity. The price disparity between rural incomes and rural house prices is now so big that, as Mrs Thatcher said in another context, there is no alternative.

Rural housing: consent or imposition?

"Villagers are much more supportive of development, ten houses here or there, to keep the pub or the school open." (Participant at the CPRE Kent focus group, April 2017)

New rural housing, including affordable housing, is often opposed, but I do not think that this is generally a result of snobbery. More often, it is down to the usual concerns about any development: that it will be imposed, poorly designed, lack adequate infrastructure and damage the local environment. Above all, as I shall explain, it is likely to arise from the fact that affordable housing usually comes as part of a package together with market housing that is neither needed nor wanted.

However, the context of the debate has changed over the last few years and there is now much greater support for house building everywhere. One picks this up from conversations, media commentary and opinion surveys. According to a 2017 National Housing Federation (NHF) survey, support for house building almost doubled in England between 2010 and 2016. Seventy-three per cent of people supported 'building homes that local people on average income can afford'. There was 65% support for new affordable housing among those living in rural areas; 68% among homeowners; and 77% among those aged 55 and above. The highest support was for 'homes from social landlords', a careful formulation: housing associations are classed as social landlords but most of the homes they build these days are not for social rent (National Housing Federation, 2017a).

This declared support for house building may not be quite the 'demise of the Nimby' proclaimed in the report's title. It is easy to say that one supports house building; the test comes when new houses are proposed for a specific place. This is particularly so in rural areas.

In the town I live in, there is a lot of building going on. Houses built just across the road shortly before we moved in were welcomed by our neighbours. We can see more houses being built from our back windows. You expect development in a large town. However, villages are different: propose new homes in a village and you are likely to get trouble. Some villages have not seen new houses for years (which is part of the problem). One reason is that there used to be a presumption on the part of planners that small rural settlements are, by their nature, unsustainable. It took 12 years to get permission to build the homes on the Stourhead Estate referred to earlier. The local authority repeatedly rejected the proposal on the grounds that the site was 'in the open countryside ... remote from services and employment'.[3] In fact, the homes, which I have visited, are within the village and occupied by people employed locally but unable to afford market housing.

There is an environmental issue about expanding villages, building in a dependency on fossil fuels when we need radical action to cut carbon emissions. But there are ways of reducing the environmental footprint of rural communities. Simply declaring that villages are 'unsustainable' is a crude response to the challenges we face. With the right policies, their environmental footprint can be reduced even as they grow (see Box 3.1). Certainly, organic growth of the sort that has characterised villages for centuries will increase their *social* sustainability.

Box 3.1: Energy efficiency

Houses in the country tend to be older than those in towns and more expensive to heat. The countryside is colder than the town, and many rural homes rely on oil for heating. However, despite the fact that they face higher than average energy costs, rural communities get little of the public money available for energy efficiency. Rural areas are home to almost a fifth of England's population but receive less than a penny for every pound that the government invests in energy efficiency (CPRE, 2015). Research by CPRE and National Energy Action shows that rural areas are five years behind urban areas in the energy efficiency of homes. On average, rural people pay 55% more to heat their homes, meaning that bills are higher by over £450 a year (Tapper, 2017).

We should do much more to retrofit old houses and improve their energy efficiency. We must also stop building new houses that leach energy. The 2015 government's decision to drop the zero-carbon homes policy was strikingly boneheaded. The house-building industry generally resists higher standards,[4] but, in this case, there was no great lobby by the industry and no serious argument that energy efficiency was slowing house building.

The Climate Change Committee's 2017 report to Parliament highlighted the fact that carbon emissions from the UK's building stock are rising. Improvements in energy efficiency (some of them fiercely contested) have saved the typical UK household around £290 a year since 2008, more than offsetting the cost of shifting to low-carbon electricity and improving energy efficiency.

Funding for energy efficiency was cut and the zero-carbon homes policy axed as part of David Cameron's war on 'green crap'. Now, the government is starting to make good its mistakes. The Clean Growth Strategy announced in October 2017 made a commitment to supporting off-grid rural communities to access greener energy. More generally, it set targets for retrofitting all existing homes (though with no details of how this will be done) and for tightening the building regulations (without explicitly bringing back the zero-carbon target for all new homes). Much more can and should be done to improve energy efficiency, particularly in rural areas. Now, perhaps, it will be.

Local plans banning development in villages are largely a thing of the past. What has not changed is the need to win over passionate and often well-qualified local people (many of them incomers), who assume that new houses will harm their village and the countryside around it. This fear is often justified; even if the development is done well, it will bring change, and people generally move to a village because they like it the way it is. However, there is plenty of evidence that when people are properly engaged and given a say, they can be persuaded to embrace development. Government statistics, albeit based on a tiny sample, suggest that neighbourhood plans result in 10% more housing than was allocated in the local plan (DCLG, 2016c).

The assumption behind neighbourhood planning is that people are not Nimbys and will embrace change if they have some say over it. This appears to be the case with my brother's village, Wymondham in Leicestershire. There, the neighbourhood plan proposes to increase the size of the parish from 281 houses to at least 344 by 2036, a bigger increase than that proposed in the draft local plan. The village's willingness to support more housing is partly a result of the process of developing the plan, which ensured that all voices could be heard, not just the loudest. However, the willingness to accept higher numbers also comes from a sense that if it does not, the village will be vulnerable to arbitrary development within a few years. Wymondham's allocation in the draft local plan has fluctuated and, as a member of the parish council put it to me, the village did not want to be "at the mercy of the scant protections offered by the NPPF [National Planning Policy Framework]".

Neighbourhood planning wins support for new housing partly because people realise that if they do not embrace development, they will get it on someone else's terms. There is a bargain here: come up with the numbers and you will be protected from arbitrary development. This should extend to villages genuinely working to produce a plan. Too often, permission is given for developments that contradict an emerging neighbourhood plan. Communities who have started to develop a neighbourhood plan that commits to development should be given at least 12 months to complete it before permission is given for speculative developments. If necessary, they should get extra support to complete the plan within this demanding timescale.

Effective engagement is hard work and requires some trust. It also means (NHF take note) not insulting those you want on your side: the knee-jerk impulse of some housing campaigners to dismiss as a 'Nimby' anyone questioning development is counterproductive.

How to do rural housing

Hastoe, England's leading specialist rural housing association, has built in over 250 villages, always with the consent of the community. Chief Executive Sue Chalkley explains how it operates:

Hastoe's development process starts with a phone call from a Parish Council.... The scheme is designed in collaboration with the community. The process is slower but the result is a proud and strengthened community as well as beautiful homes for local families. (Lloyd, 2016: 14)

Alongside most other rural housing associations, Hastoe has a 'rural pledge'. It is intended to reassure communities that small, specialist housing associations retain the social ethos of the housing association movement and have not followed the commercial path of some large housing associations. The promise is to:

- work closely with the local community and parish council to find the right site;
- always give qualifying local people in housing need first priority;
- ensure that affordable homes always remain affordable;
- build sensitively designed, high-quality homes to high environmental standards;
- provide good-quality and locally sensitive management services to residents;
- always respond positively to the local community.[5]

This sort of thing is usually PR-speak, but I think Hastoe lives by its pledge. One of my proudest moments at CPRE was being asked to open a Hastoe development of seven affordable homes in Holne, Dartmoor. The scheme took years to get off the ground. The parish first agreed that it needed some affordable homes in the late 1990s. A housing group was set up in 2007 to deliver them, and in 2010, Hastoe was called in. There was some local opposition (though CPRE Devon supported it) and the first design for the scheme had to be changed before a planning application was finally submitted in January 2013 and swiftly agreed by the National Park Authority.

The whole process took years, but then it should not be easy to build in a National Park. It is worth the effort to get it right and win consent. Hastoe's seriousness about quality and community engagement means that it is often invited back to build more homes. In Burwell, Cambridgeshire, for instance, Hastoe built 39 houses in three phases between 1994 and 2008 and has now been invited back to build 14 more dwellings (Walker, 2016: 19).

The viability game

All this is a stark contrast to how most villages experience proposals for new housing. Affordable housing is now generally funded through Section 106 agreements, which require developers to fund community benefits as a condition of planning permission. The trouble is, having been granted planning permission, they often tell the local authority that they can no longer meet these obligations. It is no longer viable, they say, to build the number of affordable homes that they had previously agreed.

Paragraph 173 of the National Planning Policy Framework (NPPF) more or less guarantees that developers will pay too much for land and then wriggle out of the commitments that won them planning permission. It states that 'to ensure viability', a development should provide 'competitive returns' to a landowner and developer (DCLG, 2012). For house builders, a competitive return means profits of at least 20%, so developers know that they will be able to avoid building affordable homes or building to high standards on grounds of non-viability (Burroughs, 2015a). The calculation of viability is complex and opaque; developers generally plead commercial confidentiality, though the Mayor of London and some London boroughs are trying to open up the process. Everyone knows that the house builders will not be made to build as many homes as they promise, so land prices are inflated. As Catharine Banks (2017) of Shelter says, developers factor in the ability to negotiate down their planning obligations when calculating how much to pay for land. 'At the heart of this debate', she says, 'is an awkward question: how is it that we have reached a point where affordable housing is seen as a cost which can be squeezed, but developer and landowner returns are fixed and non-negotiable?'

The price of developers' economic viability (or high profits) is the social viability of communities. In the rural context, research published by CPRE in June 2017 (CPRE, 2017b) shows that the proportion of affordable homes provided by non-metropolitan local authorities halved between 2011 and 2016. In 2011/12, 35% of new homes in shire districts and unitary authorities were classed as affordable; by 2015/16, the figure was just 16%.

Only five of the 15 most unaffordable districts outside London met their affordable housing target. In Epping Forest, which is 92% Green Belt and the 10th most expensive borough outside London, just 14% of new housing over the five-year period was affordable, against a target of 40%. To repeat a point made throughout this book, we are not talking here about social housing; 'affordable' housing is unaffordable to very many people. A pattern has emerged, by no means limited to rural authorities, of developers reneging on commitments to build affordable housing. In Horsham, West Sussex, an American real estate investment trust said that it could meet only half the council's 35% target for affordable housing. Faced with the prospect of an appeal or seeing the development cancelled and losing its five-year land supply, the council waved through the 2,750-home development.

A small industry (one might call it an 'anti-cottage industry') has grown up to advise developers and landowners on how to escape their commitments to fund affordable housing. S106 Management,[6] for instance, offers to help developers if their profit margin drops below 17.5%. Greenfield sites, including rural exception sites,[7] offer a particular problem, it says: 'This is because the uplift in value (from agricultural use) achieved on the grant of planning permission will in most cases support the provision of some Affordable Housing.' What a terrible thing! The firm offers to help get round this problem. Examples on its website in June 2017 included making only 'a modest contribution to affordable housing', instead of the 40% required in policy, in a scheme of 10 new houses within the Green Belt near Virginia Water, Surrey. The firm's work apparently saved £730,541. The saving for getting out of a 40% affordability requirement in Redruth, Cornwall, is quoted as £4 million.

There is no shortage of others in this business. But the problem is not the spivs; it is the system that encourages spivvery. The system is designed to favour developers while giving the appearance of local control. It was devised after the 2010 election, during the housing slump. In opposition, the Conservatives had promised to end regional planning and top-down housing targets: local people would be given the power to decide how much housing their area needed. The trouble was that no one was building. Funding for affordable housing had been slashed and the private sector house builders, having overpaid for land in the boom years, were in a very poor state. Many smaller firms went bust.

It is therefore understandable that the government bent over backwards to shore up the house-building industry. However, as it skewed the planning system in favour of developers and against both those in housing need and communities seeking to protect the countryside, it pretended that 'localism' guided planning decisions. I could never quite work out whether ministers really believed their rhetoric.

In any case, the continuing focus on housing numbers puts councils in a weak position in negotiating with developers. If the developer threatens to down tools, the local authority risks losing its five-year land supply and having its plan declared invalid. The 'presumption in favour of sustainable development' (NPPF, para 14, DCLG, 2012) then kicks in, giving the local authority very little say over what is built where. So, councils cave in; developers build fewer affordable homes and virtually no social housing; and local CPRE and other groups dig deeper into their trenches, resisting even good proposals for new housing because they assume them to be based on lies. It would be nice to report an upside: the building of more homes in total. However, this does not seem to happen either. More homes are built on greenfield sites, but not more homes in total.

"In my village, there was a proposal for a small development on a derelict pig farm. It was a good idea – the village was ageing and needed new life. The aim was a few small houses for local people. But the developer renegotiated the Section 106 agreement and reduced the number of affordable houses. It's this sort of thing that makes people disillusioned."

"There's no trust. Time after time after time, promises of schools and doctors don't materialise."

"Where are the Section 106 compliance officers?" (Participants at CPRE Leicestershire focus group, April 2017)

Second homes

Of course she knew the village was dead. Submerged beneath the rich weekenders, who never passed the time of day with the local people. Came looking for *The Woodlanders* of Thomas Hardy and then cut down the trees. (*Last friends* by Jane Gardam, 2013: 125)

In March 2013, I was on holiday just over the Welsh border in Montgomeryshire, at a big family party celebrating my mother's 80th birthday. On the Saturday, I wandered into a newsagent's in Oswestry. Glancing down at the papers, I saw a big headline on the front page of the *Times*: 'Tax "townies" out of second homes to save the countryside', it read. Interesting, I thought. Very interesting, I thought, when I read the first line of the article: 'The owners of second homes should be taxed so hard that they give up their rural retreats, the head of the Campaign to Protect Rural England has demanded.'

The story came from an interview with CPRE's President, Sir Andrew Motion. Andrew later told me that he only spent a minute giving his personal views on second homes but his words were irresistibly quotable: 'They're townies in the countryside', he said, 'they make sure they're back in London in time to catch the 10 o'clock news on Sunday night.' They 'scoot down in their cars, see their smart friends, don't join in the life of the community and don't feed into it'. The result, he said, was 'inert' dormitories, 'gutted' communities.[8]

This was not quite the party line. CPRE's policy on housing, agreed earlier that month, had a rather bland approach to second homes. It noted that they were a problem in places where 'villages and towns can be almost deserted for much of the year'. However, the remedy fell short of taxing second homeowners till the pips squeaked: local authorities should 'use the tools available to them, especially the ability to charge up to 100% Council Tax on second homes' (CPRE, 2013: para 8.6).

There was not much I could do about the *Times* story while I was in Wales, but when I got back to work a week later, it was to lots of angry letters and emails, some cancelling legacy pledges and standing orders. This was very regrettable but I had some sympathy with Andrew's comments. Second homes can suck the life out of the community. Go to Broadway in the Cotswolds on a winter's evening and it is like … well, it is like visiting one of the new luxury tower blocks in London: the lights are off.

There is always something obscene about people enjoying great wealth while others have nothing, but this is accentuated when one is talking about something as fundamental as housing. If we have a housing crisis, if 'something must be done', what about those who have more housing than they can possibly need? The egalitarian argument is made by Danny Dorling (2014) in *All that is solid*. He argues that the supply of dwellings has never been higher: 'We have more housing in Britain – more homes and more rooms in those homes – than we have ever had before. This is not just in absolute terms, but per family, per person' (Dorling, 2014: 191). The problem is not a shortage of housing; it is how the housing we have is shared out.

The distribution of housing gained greater salience following the Grenfell Tower fire tragedy of June 2017. Even before the fire, there was growing resentment at new homes being sold off-plan to foreign investors who might never live in them. There was also anger at the social cleansing that can result when estates are regenerated. As estates are rebuilt and improved (or taken upmarket), some leaseholders and tenants have been cleared out of their home areas. In addition, poor London families have been relocated to towns as far afield as Basildon, Luton or Milton Keynes as a result of the benefits cap. The story is told with barely contained fury by Anna Minton (2017) in *Big capital: Who is London for?*

But for all the undoubted iniquities of housing policy in London, the city retains, for now, its vibrancy and social mix. Not so villages dominated by second homes and holiday lets. They may be beautiful but, to quote Adam Nicolson's words at a CPRE seminar, who wants the beauty of a beautiful corpse? Even where second homes do not dominate a village, they tilt the age profile upwards as younger people are forced out. The 2011 census shows that the median age in rural communities increased from 42 to 45 in just 10 years; in urban areas, it increased from 36 to 37.

It is hard to get an exact figure for the number of second homes in England and Wales used for leisure, but the best estimate appears to be around 165,000 properties (This is Money, 2015). The issue of second homes in holiday locations gained added prominence when St Ives in Cornwall, with 25% second homes in 2011, up 67% since the 2001 census, voted for a neighbourhood plan that would restrict the purchase of new-build properties to permanent residents. Other parishes are looking to introduce similar restrictions. The problem, of course, is that such policies make second-hand properties even more desirable, forcing their price up.

There is, as ever, another viewpoint. Holiday homes bring money and jobs to tourist areas; I have stayed in many over the years, without guilt. Furthermore, second-homeowners have their story. After Andrew Motion's *Times* interview, the paper published letters from several protesting that they invested in the area, contributed to the community, supported local shops and traders, and so on. I heard similar stories as I rang angry CPRE members to try to dissuade them from resigning. Many were genuinely hurt to be thought of as the bad guys, rather than the lovers of the countryside and their (second) communities that they knew themselves to be. I was told that second homes had given children or grandchildren a love of the countryside, and about holiday homes that were occupied for most of the year by family members. One woman told me that she looked forward every day to a time when she would be able to move into the village where she had her second home but, for now, she had to stay in town for her career. Another had inherited the family home and looked forward to moving into it as soon as she retired. A less emotional argument was that villages have always been propped up by outsiders – as a contributor to my blog put it, 'weekenders are the new squires'.[9]

I am not convinced that investment in the local economy washes all other problems away. Many good people have good reasons for having second homes and one cannot outlaw them in a free country. But they undoubtedly exacerbate housing need and the problem is becoming worse as inequality grows and property becomes an ever-more attractive investment. According to the Resolution Foundation, between 2000–02 and 2012–14, the number of people owning multiple properties in the UK rose by 1.6 million. Just over 5 million people now own more than one property, one in 10 of the adult population. These second- and third-homeowners tend to be wealthy baby boomers living in the South and East of England (Resolution Foundation, 2017).

The increase in the number of people owning more than one home has, of course, coincided with a significant fall in the number who own a home at all. Second-home ownership can no longer be considered a sideshow; it is a significant contributor to the housing crisis.

Politicians have started to tackle the issue. Most local authorities in second-home hot spots now charge them 100% council tax; in 2016, a 3% stamp duty surcharge for second homes came into effect; and in 2017, tax relief for buy-to-let landlords was reduced. In rural areas, more St Ives-style neighbourhood plans will help ensure that at least some homes remain available for local people, as will ensuring that most new homes are built for local people and remain affordable in perpetuity. Ultimately, however, as with so many of the issues discussed in this book, the root of the problem is growing inequality. That cannot be tackled through housing policy alone.

'Plonking'

Up to now, this chapter has been concerned with new housing in villages. However, most opposition to development has nothing to do with whether people want more housing in and for their village. The objection is not village housing, but, in David Cameron's words, to a 'great big housing estate being plonked down from above'. Cameron said he wanted to make it easier for villages to say 'yes' to new homes for local people, and neighbourhood planning has, indeed, made it easier for communities to support new housing. But he did not stop the plonkers, and neither has his successor.[10]

Indeed, as prime minister, Cameron turned a blind eye to the consequences of his housing and planning policies. For much of his premiership, the only leverage CPRE achieved was through the pressure of backbench Conservative MPs. Some understood what was happening in their patch, the gap between the rhetoric of localism and the reality of imposition; some simply feared losing support to the United Kingdom Independence Party (UKIP).

"There's a well-known local politician who, when he became Prime Minister, said that we hadn't got to worry about planning because they didn't intend to build a hundred houses on the outskirts of villages without the permission and the approval of the people who lived there. That is precisely what is happening, of course."

"It didn't happen in his village because he bought the fields."[11]
(Participants at CPRE Oxfordshire focus group, May 2017)

Plonking has caused considerable loss of countryside and even more local strife. The Office for National Statistics (ONS) 2011 Rural–Urban Classification for Small Area Geographies shows that more than 1,300 villages in England and Wales, mostly in Southern England, disappeared in the first decade of the century. According to the report, the declassification of a village 'usually occurred where a town or city's fringe expanded.... Rarely did it result from "organic growth" of a village' (Bibby and Brindley, 2013: 20). There will have been no let-up in the rate of loss of villages since 2011.

> "My village has seen incremental growth through the last century or so and we would welcome further growth to keep life in the village, but incremental growth rather than a few hundred houses stuck on the edge." (Participant at CPRE Oxfordshire focus group, April 2017)

One case gained particular prominence: a scheme for 230 houses (half of them four- or five-bedroom executive homes) in the neighbouring Oxfordshire villages of Hook Norton and Bloxham. Cherwell District Council refused permission on the grounds that the development was incompatible with the emerging neighbourhood and local plans. Both the district council and the parish were clearly pro-housing and on course to meet their targets but they could not prove a five-year housing supply, so the presumption in favour of development kicked in and the secretary of state overruled them. The local MP, Sir Tony Baldry, who had previously rejected CPRE's concerns as exaggerated, said he was "angry, disappointed and frustrated". A local resident, Peter Millar, wrote in the *Sunday Times*:

> In Hook Norton and Bloxham there is a mood of sullen anger, despair and disempowerment. There is a feeling that big business, with its expensive consultants, in-house lawyers and the ear of government ministers, gets its way while people are ignored. (Millar, 2013)

Hook Norton is home to a national journalist. There are many other villages around the country that could tell a similar story.

A living countryside: the case for rural development

For all the concerns about imposition and inappropriate development, there is a strong case for more rural housing – much more in some places. This is not just about affordable housing or the organic growth of villages. If we aspire to have a living countryside, we should acknowledge that in some parts of Britain, both people and nature have all but left the land. 'There are', as Trevor Rowley (2006: 2) says, 'huge tracts of empty countryside, emptier now than they have been for thousands of years'. He quotes Gerald Woodward's 2004 novel, *I'll go to bed at noon*: 'The Great North Road had become a highway through sad prairies almost as far as Scotland. There was a sadness about that landscape, relentlessly simplified, big and empty when once it had been small and complicated' (Rowley, 2006: 265).

This prompts the question: 'What is the countryside for?' If it is both empty of people and ecologically barren, what good is it doing? The obvious answer is growing food, but much of our arable farmland is mainly used to grow feed for animals whose meat is exported (in recent years, the Department for Environment, Food and Rural Affairs [Defra] has had an obsession with selling pig meat to China). We can make our countryside more beautiful, accessible, sustainable and flood- and climate change-resistant without sacrificing food resilience. With care, new housing can benefit nature, as well as society.

To be clear, it does not follow that because an area of countryside is intensively farmed or needs improvement, it should be built over. The first priority is to improve it, and Brexit gives us the chance to do so. Over £3 billion a year is spent on land management through the Common Agricultural Policy, the vast majority in the form of direct payments to farmers. This subsidy comes with minimal environmental conditions and helps inflate land prices. We can get much better value.

Consider, for instance, the creation of the National Forest, which covers a 200-square-mile area of the East Midlands badly hit by the collapse of coal mining. Here, economic regeneration has gone hand-in-hand with nature restoration, including the planting of over 8 million trees. The total cost to the public purse from 1991 to 2010 was £89 million, a snip compared with £3 billion a year. For anyone who believes this sort of thing, the National Forest Company claims a benefits-to-cost ratio of 2.6:1 (Eftec, 2010).

The National Forest shows how countryside can be improved for both people and nature. It should not be beyond our ability to extend towns and villages, possibly even create new ones, without causing excessive harm. In the words of John Buchan, launching CPRE Oxfordshire in March 1931, "change may be all to the good if you replace old beauty with new beauty and not with new ugliness". Furthermore, even if one would prefer not to build in the countryside, bold, well-planned development would surely be preferable to what we get now: planning battles across rural England that too often result in poorly planned and poorly executed estates plonked down on the edge of towns and villages, with no benefit to rural communities or the natural world.

The trouble is that there is generally zero confidence that a new development can result in better places. Indeed, the common and justified assumption is that development causes harm; that promises of affordable housing, good design and green infrastructure will be negotiated away on grounds of non-viability; and that local people will be lied to and forced to accept whatever the developer can get away with.

It is not always like this, but it almost always seems like this to local people faced with development – development that is always framed as meeting housing numbers, rather than creating a better place. We need a radically improved system.

Notes

[1] See: www.cpre.org.uk/resources/housing-and-planning/planning/item/download/394

[2] See: www.stourhead.com/estate/images/Brook_Cottages_allocation_policy.pdf. This chapter focuses mainly on the role of rural housing associations, but private estates like the Stourhead Estate play an important role in providing affordable homes in rural areas. With the right sort of support, they could do more (Walker, 2016).

[3] See the officer's recommendation to the local planning committee in November 2014, available at: https://cms.wiltshire.gov.uk/documents/s82852/13%2000636%20FUL.pdf. The application was eventually agreed by local councillors, partly because it had strong support from the parish council.

[4] Nick Raynsford (2016: 78), recalling the house builders' resistance in the 1990s to improving building regulations, reflects on 'the considerable influence of this industry as a lobbying force'.

[5] See 'About Hastoe 2016', promotional leaflet, available at: www.hastoe.com/download/2542/About-Hastoe-2016.aspx

[6] See: www.section-106.co.uk/

[7] These are small sites, usually on the edge of villages, which would not usually be considered suitable for development. They are typically gifted or sold at near to agricultural value by the landowner in order to provide permanently affordable housing for the village.

[8] See: https://www.thetimes.co.uk/article/tax-townies-out-of-second-homes-to-save-countryside-sbvjv029hgs

[9] 'CPRE and second homes: the official position', 11 April 2013. Available at: https://cpreviewpoint.wordpress.com/2013/04/11/cpre-and-second-home-the-official-position/

[10] See *Daily Telegraph* (2012). This piece reports David Cameron telling the BBC's *Countryfile* that he would no more put at risk the countryside of West Oxfordshire 'than I would put at risk my own family'. One of his Number 10 colleagues told me shortly after this statement: "If I were his family, I'd be very worried".

[11] The jaundiced comment about David Cameron refers to the purchase of a small patch of land near his home for £140,000, see: www.telegraph.co.uk/news/politics/david-cameron/8908429/David-Cameron-in-140000-land-deal-with-lobbying-boss.html

FOUR

Why it matters where we build: environmental constraints

In November 2012, the Planning Minister, Nick Boles, told BBC *Newsnight*: 'In the UK and England at the moment we've got about 9% of land developed. All we need to do is build on another 2–3% of land and we'll have solved a housing problem.'[1] Leaving aside the detail – whether he meant England or the UK; whether 9% was the right figure for either – the insouciance with which Boles suggested building over an area of countryside the size of Cornwall was alarming. His remarks provoked a powerful (if factually wobbly) response from the high Tory philosopher Roger Scruton:

Mr Boles tells us that only 7 per cent [sic] of our country is built upon, so what harm to add another 3 per cent? But much that is not built on is mountainous or uninhabitable. The small remainder has been protected for 100 years by legislation – not as an economic concern, but as an immovable part of what we are. Take away that 3 per cent, and you take away the heart of England. (*Daily Telegraph*, 1 December 2012)

I am on Scruton's side, but Boles had a point: most of the UK, even most of the South-East of England is remarkably undeveloped. For a politician whose main concern is to get stuff built, all that land with development potential, seemingly doing nothing very much, represents a failure. For others, the fact that our rich, crowded country has managed to retain so much countryside is something to celebrate.

It is also a reason to avoid scaremongering about its loss. That is why in my time at the Campaign to Protect Rural England (CPRE) I tried to ban the evocative phrase, 'concreting over the countryside'. Travel around most of England and it is clear that we are far from losing the countryside to concrete.

But that is not to deny the fact that we are losing large areas of countryside. CPRE regularly reports that an area of countryside the size of such-and-such city is being lost each year. For instance, government figures show that in 2015/16, 15,405 hectares of greenfield land were developed, an area over twice the size of Nottingham.[2] Until 2010, the government had a target that at least 60% of new housing should be built on brownfield land. This was comfortably exceeded for years. The Coalition abolished the target and over 50% of new houses are now built on greenfield land. Yes, there is a good deal of countryside left, but it is not scaremongering to raise the alarm about losses on this scale.

Arguments will continue about what percentage or acreage of countryside we are losing and how much is left, but what is at stake is deeply emotional: 'the heart of England'. People care about the character of the countryside and the harm done by specific developments to specific places. Those who love a piece of countryside will be left heartbroken by its loss, and I am always surprised when enthusiasts for development seem unable to understand this. Instead, they often glibly reassure that they have no desire to build over the *best* countryside. National Parks, Areas of Outstanding Natural Beauty (AONBs), nature reserves and so on will be safe, on the whole. What they have in their sights are small plots of nondescript, scrubby countryside and monocultural farmland – just two or three percent more.

"I was at a meeting at Barton last night, which is, for Oxfordshire, a comparatively deprived community. There's a high percentage of social housing. The passion in that room for protecting the countryside on their doorstep was unbelievable. Those who don't have choices about where they live have got an even greater incentive to make that community work and to protect it. There was a real strong sense of community there and a real passion for protecting the character of that community and the landscape in which it sits.

"When you've got a 21-year-old living in a mobile home stating that she does not want development on the Green Belt because it won't help her housing but she will lose her quality of life, that's pretty powerful. Our messages – they're not getting through as CPRE, she'd never heard of CPRE before, but she was giving out CPRE messages." (Participant at CPRE Oxfordshire focus group, May 2017)

The two or three percent more approach fails to appreciate three things. First, there is a development halo: development in rural areas has a big impact on the character of the surrounding countryside. Second, places casually dismissed as uninteresting or unattractive and therefore ripe for development have qualities to which the boosters for development are often blind: they matter. Third, there is a particular issue about 'distressed' countryside on the urban fringe. It is easy to say that it is worthless and should be built on, but there is an alternative: improvement through creating new forests, country parks or nature reserves. Furthermore, where improvement is not possible, untidy countryside on the edge of towns can be accepted and even celebrated.

I will consider these three points in turn. The focus here is on Green Belt and the 'ordinary', unprotected countryside. It should not be thought, however, that even the most protected countryside is free from development pressures. For instance, between 2012 and 2017, there was a fivefold increase in the amount of AONB land approved for housing each year, and a nine-fold increase in the area of land approved in the settings of AONBs. (CPRE, 2017c: 3, 4). There were over 60 applications of 10 units or more in the Cotswolds AONB alone, and more and more applications are being approved by local authorities or taken to appeal by developers (Dixon et al, 2017: 8)

The development halo

In a Mori survey for the 2006 Barker review of land-use planning, 54% of respondents thought that half or more of England was developed; only 13% believed that the proportion was less than a quarter. In fact, according to Kate Barker, the most developed region apart from Greater London was the South-East, with 12.2% of land developed. Gardens are counted as developed land. Barker (2006: 43) concluded that 'people have a marked tendency to overestimate the proportion of urban land in England'. However, the reason people think that more than half the country is developed is that it often feels like it. As Nicholas Schoon puts it:

> As an area or region becomes increasingly built up, it looks, sounds, feels and smells less and less like countryside. It becomes harder and harder for people – most of them living in towns and cities – to 'get away from it all' because traffic and built development are closer and closer at hand. An area can no longer be perceived as predominantly rural long before half of its surface is covered by development. (CPRE, 2005: 5)

CPRE's intrusion maps show how much of England is disturbed by noise, light, buildings, roads, overhead wires and so on. There are maps using the same methodology (devised by Land Use Consultants) for the early-1960s, the early-1990s and the mid-2000s. The maps show the speed with which undisturbed countryside has been lost, particularly in the South-East.

Figure 4.1: Intrusion map: England, early 1960s

Source: CPRE and Countryside Commission (2007a), based on Ordnance Survey Information with the permission of The Controller of Her Majesty's Stationery Office.

Figure 4.2: Intrusion map: England, 2007

Source: CPRE and Countryside Commission (2007b), based on Ordnance Survey Information with the permission of The Controller of Her Majesty's Stationery Office.

In Medway, Kent, for instance, where I live, 62% of the district was undisturbed by noise or visual intrusion in the early 1960s. By the early 1990s, the figure was down to 46%. By the time the 2007 maps had been produced, only 24% was undisturbed. This loss of tranquillity is not all down to housing and there have been gains as well as losses, for instance, nature reserves along the river where there used to be industry. But it is a sobering fact that an area that was predominantly rural has, within a couple of generations, lost that character. There is wonderful countryside in and around Medway, but little of it is now undisturbed, particularly by traffic noise. It is therefore unsurprising that the first instinct of many people will be to oppose new housing. However needed, it will inevitably erode what is left of the area's rural character.

Box 4.1: The love of place

I live in Rochester, on the River Medway, so trying to explain why the North Kent marshes and Hoo Peninsula are special opens me to the charge of Nimbyism. Well, so be it. There is plenty of development going on in and around Rochester and I welcome most of it. However, there is something about this strange, wild stretch of countryside that is extraordinarily precious. It is neither undeveloped nor conventionally beautiful. The marks of past activities are everywhere – broken barges, abandoned forts, gravel pits. There is also some pretty unattractive 20th-century housing – bungalows and the sort of estates that gave council housing a bad name.

In spite of this the Hoo Peninsula is largely rural, mostly farmland, and rich in history. It inspired the opening scene of *Great expectations*, where Magwitch first meets, and terrifies, Pip. It is also relatively empty, near to London, and poor. This makes it a target for development and it is clear that its population would benefit from the right sort of investment. Too often, however, it is seen, to quote a Historic England guide, as 'a blank canvas upon which major changes can take place without consequence for its historic character and the way that character benefits the people who live, work and spend time there' (Newsome et al, 2015: 74). Boris Johnson wanted to build his Boris Island airport here. In 2014, Shelter proposed a new garden city with a population of 100,000 or more (the current population of the Hoo Peninsula is 31,000, and that of Stoke village, the site of the proposed new city, just over 1,000).[3]

Most worryingly, Medway Council wants to build 5,000 homes at Lodge Hill, a Site of Special Scientific Interest and the most important home for breeding nightingales in the country. One does not need to have heard a nightingale sing or be a fan of John Keats or Vera Lynn to object. This remarkable proposal keeps being knocked back, but both Medway's Tory council and its Labour opposition are keen on it. If it ever happens, it really will be open season for nature in England.

None of this is meant to suggest that Hoo should not develop. It always has, and as industry changes and its power stations become obsolete, there will be more schemes proposed, all no doubt claiming to alleviate its deprivation. Shelter's proposal was well-considered, economically viable given the political will and, apparently, popular with focus groups of local people. However, more than trebling the population on a peninsula with one main road off it that is already choked at rush hour ... really?

My real point here is not to argue the pros and cons of building a garden city on the Hoo Peninsula. It is that even scruffy, distressed, apparently unprepossessing places like Hoo and the North Kent marshland can have a rich history that should be respected. Carol Donaldson, retreading a walk taken by William Hogarth in 1732, sees 'something unchanging in the Thames and what's left of the marshes and fields. It is easy to strip away the layers of modern life here, the past is always visible like a wash under oil paint' (Donaldson, 2017b: np). It is worth protecting partly because it is a wild area on the doorstep of the crowded Medway towns: untamed, unmanicured countryside, without all the waymarks and information boards one gets in the nearby (and excellent) country parks. We should tread carefully because of its rich history, and we should treasure it for its strange beauty.

People also want towns to retain their identity. The Adam Smith Institute's Tom Papworth (2015: 24), recalling how the growth of 19th-century Manchester overwhelmed surrounding settlements, observes that 'a similar process has seen the merger of Chatham, Maidstone, Rainham and Rochester, home to more than a quarter of a million people'. But this is not true. These towns are under pressure and Rochester and Chatham, in particular, bump up against each other. Even so, the Medway towns retain their distinct identities and Maidstone is in a separate borough, physically separated by the North Downs. The Downs may be an inconvenient fact for the Adam Smith Institute, but they are a joy to others.

The erosion of Medway's rural character is not exceptional. In the early 1960s, 22% of East Sussex was disturbed; by the time the 2007 maps were produced, the figure was 56%. West Sussex went from 30% disturbed to 65%, and Surrey from 58% to 85%.[4] CPRE Surrey is one of CPRE's most protectionist branches, and given the development pressures it faces, it has to be. Housing campaigners point out that there are 142 golf courses in Surrey and, as someone who dislikes golf and golf courses, I cannot rejoice in that. In some ways, I would prefer houses. However, building houses over Surrey's golf courses would be a good way to destroy what little undisturbed countryside the county still enjoys, not because golf courses are proper countryside (they are not), but because housing has a much bigger footprint in terms of the roads, shops, services, lighting and so on that comes with it.[5]

Urban intrusion is not limited to the South-East. Between the early 1960s and 2007, Leeds district went from 76% to 97% disturbed; I doubt it now has any undisturbed countryside left. Even North Yorkshire, the least disturbed part of Yorkshire and Humber, went from an intrusion level of 8% to 27%.[6] Warwickshire went from 33% to 66%, Worcestershire from 27% to 60%[7] and so on. In regional terms, the South-West went from 15% to 42% disturbed, and the East of England from 29% to 50%. There are still undisturbed parts of the country, but they are getting harder to find.

Many cities have lost their last oases of undisturbed countryside. Between the 1960s and 2007, the district of Kingston-upon-Hull lost its last 7%. The same is true of Birmingham, Coventry, Liverpool, Manchester, Salford, Blackpool, Bolton, Bournemouth, Poole and many other towns and cities, north to south. I know this phenomenon is not new, but we should think carefully about what is lost, as well as gained, by development, and acknowledge that the impact of new housing reverberates far beyond the area of land that is actually built on.

Places matter

> Behind every generalization, there lies the infinite variety and
> beauty of detail; and it is the detail that matters, that gives
> pleasure to the eye and to the mind, as we traverse, on foot
> and unhurried, the landscape of any part of England. (Hoskins,
> 1979 [1955]: 210)

It is hard for anyone writing about the English landscape to resist
quoting W.G. Hoskins's 1955 masterpiece, *The making of the English
landscape* (Hoskins, 1979 [1955]), and I would not want to. Hoskins
saw landscape as a palimpsest containing layer after layer of history,
'depths beyond depths in the simplest scene' (Hoskins, *Midland England*,
quoted in Samuel, 1994: 187). He encourages us to read the landscapes
around us, quiet or unprepossessing landscapes as well as the most feted.
The Lake District might be a great symphony, but 'there is as much
pleasure to be had in the chamber music of Bedfordshire or Rutland;
perhaps, one might say, a more sophisticated pleasure in discovering
the essence of these simpler and smaller landscapes' (Hoskins, 1979
[1955]: 20) Hoskins feared that the sheer scale of modern landscape
transformation was not so much adding a new layer to the historical
record, as destroying all that went before. The last chapter of his book
is a howl of rage at the obliteration of our past. Since the Industrial
Revolution, he said, and especially since 1914, 'every single change in
the English landscape has either uglified it or destroyed its meaning,
or both ... let us turn away and contemplate the past before all is lost
to the vandals' (Hoskins, 1979 [1955]: 298–9).

Of course, some find it possible (as Hoskins did not) to 'contemplate
without pain' major landscape change. The geographer Brian Short
(2006: 242), for instance, remarks that 'yesterday's landscape destruction
or urban sprawl will sooner or later become tomorrow's heritage'.
Well, maybe. But to paraphrase Keynes, sooner or later, we are all
dead. Conservationists understand that the buildings and landscapes
they fight to protect have changed over time, but that does not make
them any less precious.

No one captures better than Bill Bryson the sense that all of the English countryside is special and should be treasured. It is, he says, 'an exceptional creation – a corner of the world that is immensely old, full of surprises, lovingly and sometimes miraculously well maintained, and nearly always pleasing to look at' (Bryson, 2000: 1–2).

> Nowhere on earth, surely, is there greater diversity and interest packed into a smaller area. You really can't go five miles in England without encountering some quite extraordinary diversion – a folly, ruin, ancient stone circle, Iron Age fort or some other striking reminder of the depth and busyness of the country's past. (Bryson, 2000: 5)

Bryson, who was CPRE President from 2007 to 2012, argues that the whole of the English countryside should be protected as a National Park. We have, he says, been endowed with one of the loveliest landscapes the world has ever known: 'The real work is done. All that is required of you is to look after it. That doesn't seem too much to ask' (Bryson, 2000: 13).

The idea is appealing. It reminds us to proceed with care. A greenfield housing development may be necessary, it may even be beautiful, but it will also involve loss. A field is never just a field; it can be a place for recreation, a miniature nature reserve, a repository of history. Anna Pavord lists some of the field names in an 1839 tithe map of Powerstock parish in South-West Dorset, 'witnesses to the continuity that marks the gradual occupation of land in Britain, for it is the fields that make our landscape so intimate, so diverse, so particular': Puzzicks, Flinty Nap, Bellringer's Orchard, Marsh Mead, Bean Close, Cowleaze, Roper's Quarry, Marl Pits, Pig's Plot, Starvelands, Foans, Drang (Pavord, 2016: 189). These could, I suppose, provide the names for cul-de-sacs in some new housing development ('Starveland Pastures', perhaps). But anyone looking at the countryside around Powerstock (just five miles from growing Bridport) misses something vital if they see only development potential.

Small patches of countryside, scrubby or beautiful, can also protect a place's identity. I recall a national CPRE trustee visiting a village to support a campaign against a new housing development and feeling that the battle was already lost: this was not *real* countryside, just a couple of fields separating a village from its nearest town. However, for the villagers, those fields were crucial. They knew that they were beleaguered, but they wanted to continue living in a village (one listed in the Domesday Book, indeed) not a suburb. Many villages fear that they are going to be engulfed, and they will not be consoled by being told that this has happened throughout history.

"Oxfordshire is one of the most rural counties in the south of England. I've lived and worked here for 40-odd years and I've chosen to do that because it is a rural county. You're very close to the countryside.... We live in a very privileged place within striking distance of Oxford, the River Thames, the Chilterns and the Cotswolds. We can jump on a train and within an hour, be up in London. That is very blessed, I guess, but we would like to preserve it." (Participant at CPRE Oxfordshire focus group, April 2017)

For Roger Scruton, the shared love of home ('oikophilia', as he rather unappealingly calls it) is 'the only serious resource that we have, in our fight to maintain local order in the face of globally stimulated decay', the best hope of winning battles for the environment. It is, indeed, a powerful motivator, and one that environmentalists should take more seriously (Scruton, 2012: 25–6). Climate change and the global loss of biodiversity are the world's great environmental challenges, but such is their immensity that they often provoke unhelpful emotions: fear, boredom, helplessness or, particularly among men of a certain age, hostility. They lack political bite. The environmental cause that wins or loses parliamentary seats is the defence of places people love. Whether you call it 'oikophilia' or, like Fiona Reynolds (2016), 'the fight for beauty', the sense of place is a powerful motivator. Start there and you have a hope of connecting with the larger, global issues.

England in particular[8]

Around 10 years ago, I visited Bruton in Somerset to see an exhibition by students from the London School of Architecture. Bruton was used as a case study of how a small town could be improved by infill. The students' ideas and designs were inspiring, but the local authority, covering 370 square miles, had no capacity to promote such schemes or find suitable infill sites. Like all councils under all recent governments, its job was to meet housing targets, and the easiest way to do this was to give planning permission for big, greenfield sites.

Having seen the exhibition, I was driven down the road to just such a site, a new development of executive homes on the edge of the town. The houses were not really part of the town and there was no pavement allowing residents to walk to it. Parking spaces are at a premium in Bruton, so residents tended to drive in the opposite direction to shop. The new houses looked the same as the houses tacked onto market towns across England, which is not surprising as big builders use the same house styles from Land's End to John O'Groats. Pattern books are nothing new, but the Georgian pattern books were both fairly localised and architecturally first-rate. No one could say either of the homes we build now.

This depressing development was called The Pastures. A Google search in October 2017 revealed recent developments with the same name in Kent, Essex, Lancashire, Hampshire, North Yorkshire, Cleveland, Buckinghamshire and, curiously, North London. Presumably, the land over which they were built was once pasture.

> "Adverts for houses may say 'delightful village' but they say much more about the road and rail connections. Some people with children buy into the village community, but many don't. They just want a convenient place to base themselves." (Participant at CPRE Leicestershire focus group)

If for no other reason than to get people to support new housing, we should aim to build homes that will give pleasure to future generations, which enhance places rather than degrade them. Bland, anywhere developments turn people against new housing. Local distinctiveness is one of this country's joys. When the poet U.A. Fanthorpe writes in 'Earthed' that 'this narrow island charged with echoes/ And whispers snares me', she is thinking of its local peculiarity – like 'Somerset belfries, so highly/ Parochial that Gloucestershire has none'.[9] English villages and market towns are generally attractive and invariably rich in history; every careless development risks damaging something special.

England packs a good deal of difference into a small space and we should treasure its variety. This was the theme of *England in particular*, the charity Common Ground's celebration of 'the distinctive details that cumulatively make England' and 'counterblast against loss and uniformity' (Clifford and King, 2006). Half a century earlier, Ian Nairn wrote *Outrage*, the most famous post-war polemic against the blandification and suburbanisation of Britain:

> The Outrage is that the whole land surface is being covered by the creeping mildew that already circumscribes all of our towns. The death by slow decay we have called Subtopia, a compound word formed from suburb and utopia, i.e. making an ideal of suburbia.

The symptom of Subtopia 'will be … that the end of Southampton will look like the beginning of Carlisle; the parts in between will look like the end of Carlisle or the beginning of Southampton'.[10]

Clearly, poor design and disregard for local character is nothing new. However, one can acknowledge changing tastes and still be appalled by the poor design and indifference to place of much of the housing being built today. Not all of it, of course. There are some outstanding contemporary developments, the best of which reinterpret the vernacular and give it a modern form. However, too many appear to be thrown up with no thought to quality or place.

"What's making some of these places seem undesirable, is you're doing strategic sites of 200 houses, 600 houses, all looking the same in the same bricks. They say, 'we're looking at design' and they write a nice document which is advisory, but the result is the equivalent of the Birmingham back-to-backs for the rural countryside in what is still, and one hopes to keep, a decent looking countryside with good houses where they are built in a phased way, such that the communities can develop, the way towns develop in a natural way. That's not the way building is happening." (Participant in CPRE Oxfordshire focus group, May 2017)

Attention to local character can have surprising results. In 2015, CPRE Sussex and Action in Rural Sussex (the county's rural community council) held workshops in seven parishes to explore how development could 'create attractive, affordable and lively places' (CPRE Sussex, no date). One of the workshops took place in Peacehaven, a place loathed by CPRE's pioneers as a bungaloid excrescence. Bungalows, wrote Clough Williams-Ellis (1996: 141–2), 'constitute England's most disfiguring disease ... our premier epidemic.... Peacehaven may still be cited as the classic example of the ravages of this distressing and almost universal complaint'. However, almost a century after Peacehaven's first construction phase, the conclusion of CPRE's workshop was to respect the place's special character. This means supporting some densification (the context of the workshop was the recognition that Sussex will have to accommodate a good deal of house building) but maintaining the grid and the fact that Peacehaven was planned for bungalows.

The same attention to local character applies at least as much in more rural and (I insist) more beautiful villages. A 1996 CPRE pamphlet, *Local attraction* (McGhie and Girling, 1996: 3), argues for housing that is 'designed to enhance the landscape rather than simply to squat on it'. It gives the example of Thorncombe in West Dorset, where 'diehard' villagers had thwarted various attempts to build new housing. By working with the community, local planners got agreement for 75 new homes, compared with the 50 units that villagers had previously opposed. It was not development that they were against, but 'the misplaced suburban ethic of the volume house builders'. A high-quality development was made possible by the council's insistence on capping the cost of land as a condition of planning permission. This, the pamphlet suggests, reduced the landowner's profits (compared with the price of agricultural land) from 15,000% to 11,000%, 'a sacrifice which few would consider too onerous' (McGhie and Girling, 1996: 16–17).

As a coda to this story, it is worth noting two things. First, it is much harder now for a local authority to insist on good design at the cost of lower profits for the landowner as it would almost certainly lose a planning appeal. This makes it even more important to ensure the continued availability of low-cost rural exception sites for social housing. Second, the official tourism website for Dorset notes that, 'due to its location, the parish has become increasingly popular with second home buyers'.[11] I do not know the village, but it is likely that some of the new homes that the villagers were persuaded to accept now lie empty for most of the year.

The edgelands

Countryside abutting developed areas is rarely pristine or conventionally beautiful. Marion Shoard (2002) coined the word 'edgelands' to describe this urban fringe and challenged writers to tell its story. The poets Paul Farley and Michael Symmons Roberts responded in a book celebrating 'the fringes of English towns and cities, where urban and rural negotiate and renegotiate their borders … where overspill housing estates break into scrubland, wasteland; if you know these underdeveloped, unwatched territories, you know that they have "edge"'. (Farley and Symmons Roberts, 2011: 4–5).

Such places gave CPRE's pioneers the shakes. They wanted to tidy them up, to make them clearly either town or country. This intolerance of the edgelands is shared by today's developers who want to make them part of the town, or at least of subtopia. Surely, they say, new houses would make them more attractive? The trouble is that such countryside is always hard to maintain, and unscrupulous landowners have an incentive to run it down still more if they think they can get planning permission: they will make a fortune. However, when that urban fringe is developed, the next bit of countryside becomes, well, urban fringe, and ripe for development.

In some cases, as the *Edgelands* poets argue, untidy countryside on the urban fringe should be celebrated for what it is. Apart from anything else, it is often surprisingly rich in nature. And there is also the option of improving the countryside around towns. This applies particularly to the Green Belt, the focal point for so many battles over development. It is to the Green Belt that we now turn.

Why the Green Belt is worth fighting for

> The notion of Green Belts ... is to my mind the most intelligent, far-sighted, thrillingly and self-evidently successful land management policy any nation has ever devised. (Bryson, 2015: 161–2)

The Green Belt is the best-known and most popular planning policy we have. For all Bill Bryson's rapturous praise, that might appear to be damning with faint praise, but even if people are inclined to sneer at planning generally, they tend to rally round the Green Belt. That is why a sustained and well-funded campaign to weaken Green Belt policy, backed by influential commentators from across the political spectrum, has not, so far, succeeded. The policy remains strong, though, as this section will explain, its enforcement is weak.

Green Belt is popular but often misunderstood. It is not an environmental designation (see Box 4.2) and does not have to be beautiful. Green Belt land that is unattractive, inaccessible or ecologically barren can still serve its purposes. However, it is important to be clear that much of the Green Belt is beautiful, well-used and rich in nature. Large parts of it are also designated as AONBs (eg a quarter of the Metropolitan Green Belt around London and a fifth of the Avon Green Belt around Bristol and Bath) or as Sites of Special Scientific Interest (eg the unspoilt and historically important countryside around Darwin's home, Down House in the London Borough of Bromley).

Box 4.2: What is the Green Belt?

Green Belts in their modern form were first introduced in England in the 1930s to protect the countryside around Sheffield and London. Their national designation goes back to Duncan Sandys' Green Belt Circular of 1955. Nine paragraphs long with a short annex – two sides of paper in total – this drew local authorities' attention:

> to the importance of checking the unrestricted sprawl of built-up areas, and of safeguarding the surrounding countryside against further encroachment.... The only really effective way to achieve this object is by the formal designation of clearly defined Green Belts around the areas concerned.

Sandys, Minister of Housing and Local Government, told the House of Commons on 26 April 1955: 'I am convinced that, for the well-being of our people and for the preservation of the countryside, we have a clear duty to do all we can to prevent the further unrestricted sprawl of the great cities.'[12]

There are now 13 Green Belts in England, covering around 12.5% of the country's land area. There are also Green Belts in Scotland, Wales and Northern Ireland. The National Planning Policy Framework (NPPF), which applies only to England, states in paragraph 79: 'The government attaches great importance to Green Belts. The fundamental aim of Green Belt policy is to prevent urban sprawl by keeping land permanently open; the essential characteristics of Green Belts are their openness and their permanence' (DCLG, 2012).

Paragraph 80 states:

> Green Belts serve five purposes:
>
> * to check the unrestricted sprawl of large built-up areas;
> * to prevent neighbouring towns merging into one another;
> * to assist in safeguarding the countryside from encroachment;
> * to preserve the setting and special character of historic towns; and
> * to assist in urban regeneration, by encouraging the recycling of derelict and other urban land.

These are not environmental purposes and there is no requirement for Green Belts to be of high landscape, biodiversity or amenity value. However, the often-neglected paragraph 81 of the NPPF states that local authorities should plan 'to enhance the beneficial use of the Green Belt, such as looking for opportunities to provide access ... to retain and enhance landscapes, visual amenity and biodiversity; or to improve damaged and derelict land'.

Green Belt boundaries should be altered only 'in exceptional circumstances, through the preparation or review of the Local Plan'. 'Inappropriate development' in the Green Belt should only be approved 'in very special circumstances'. The meaning of 'very special circumstances' is set out in the NPPF and the bar is quite high, though mineral extraction, engineering infrastructure and local transport are not considered inappropriate. Finally, paragraph 92 of the NPPF notes that 'Community Forests offer valuable opportunities for improving the environment around towns, by upgrading the landscape and providing for recreation and wildlife.'

The most thorough analysis of the state of the Green Belt in England was carried out by CPRE and Natural England in 2010 (CPRE, 2010). This showed that it has: 30,000 km of rights of way; 222,000 hectares of broadleaf and mixed woodland; 19% of the country's remaining ancient woodland; 33% of its local nature reserves (a disproportionately high proportion that is made possible because the Green Belt depresses land prices); 44% of the total land area of country parks; and many other good things.

The conclusion that the Green Belt is serving more than its five planning purposes was reinforced by further research in 2016 (ADAS, 2016). Thirteen percent of Green Belt land is classified as priority habitat, the most important habitat for nature conservation as identified in the UK Biodiversity Action Plan; the proportion in comparator areas, land around urban areas that is not designated as Green Belt, is 10%. The Green Belt also accounts for:

- 35% of Woodland Trust land;
- 34% of the land area of community forests;
- 23% of registered parks and gardens; and
- 17% of public rights of way, more per hectare than in comparator areas and over twice as many as in the country as a whole.

Since the earlier report, 48 local nature reserves had been created in the Green Belt.

When one considers the pressure that Green Belt land is under, it is remarkable that so much of it is of such a high quality. Read the Green Belt's critics and you could be forgiven for thinking that it consists entirely of scrubby edgelands, ecologically barren farmland, horticulture, airports and sewage farms. In fact, taken as a whole, it is a fantastic resource for both recreation and nature conservation.

Two thirds of it is farmed; this annoys its critics but we need farms and it is good to grow the food we need close to where most of us live. Farmland can be good for nature. Where it is not (and too much farmland is of low environmental quality), it should be improved.

All this suggests that the Green Belt is worth fighting for even as a resource for recreation and the environment, leaving aside its main five purposes. However, because of its location, it is also worth improving. CPRE likes to say that Green Belts provide 'the countryside next door for 30 million people', but more needs to be done to make this claim a reality. I remember trying to interest the environmental charity Groundwork in a joint project to show the value of the Green Belt to city-dwellers. Its chief executive, Tony Hawkhead, was sceptical. Go into any urban park on a Saturday afternoon, he said, and you will see hundreds of people; leave the waymarked trails in any part of the Green Belt and you can walk miles without seeing anyone. This is true. If the Green Belt is the countryside next door, many city-dwellers seem indifferent to their neighbour. Those who use it are likely to be white and well off. When the Bangladeshi family in Monica Ali's *Brick Lane* venture out of Tower Hamlets to enjoy a picnic in beautiful surroundings, they do not go east into the countryside and the Green Belt, but west to St. James's Park. That is enough of an adventure for them.

More must be done to show people the value of the Green Belt and help them get into it. We can also improve its quality. The Thames Chase Community Forest shows what can be done. Its origins lie in a planning *cause célèbre* of the mid-1980s, when it was proposed to build 5,500 houses on Green Belt land around Tillingham Hall on the eastern edge of London. This was unlovely, empty land that had been used for landfill and gravel extraction, and on the face of it, the development proposal was a good one: a new 'country town' with a high street, lakes and employment for 2,000 people.

However, it breached Green Belt policy and raised fears that if it was given the go-ahead, Upminster would gradually sprawl east until it joined Basildon, 12 miles away. CPRE Essex and others fought a spirited campaign to hold the Green Belt line, and defeated the proposal. Only once the threat of development was lifted was it was possible to create a new, better landscape: the Thames Chase Community Forest. This now covers 40 square miles. Over 2 million trees have been planted, and there are meadows, ponds, country parks, footpaths, bridleways and cycle ways. It is an inspiring creation, but its genesis lies not in a rosy vision of the future, but in the bloody-minded defence of degraded, unattractive Green Belt land. This was a fight to protect the Green Belt as a planning designation in order to check urban sprawl. The Thames Chase Community Forest is a demonstration of the positive power of saying 'no'.

There are many other examples of the transformation of poor-quality Green Belt. The Lee Valley Regional Park, four fifths of which is in the Green Belt, is a 42 km linear park serving London, Hertfordshire and Essex. Once home to gravel pits, distilleries, munitions factories and other industries, it now has country parks, nature reserves, lakes, riverside trails and, following the 2012 Olympics, world-class sports facilities. It is an extraordinary resource for people and nature in a heavily built-up area, and we would not have it without the Green Belt. Pose a choice between bitterns and houses, and houses will win. It is the inflexibility of Green Belt policy that has allowed nature to thrive in the Lee Valley.

The Mersey Forest covers over 30 times the land area of the Lee Valley Regional Park, but (being up north) has a much smaller budget (£1.4 million a year compared with £25 million). Nevertheless, it has done wonders. Bold Forest Park in St Helens, for instance, has transformed an area once dominated by colliery spoil heaps. Northwich Woodlands within the community forest is a haven for wildlife and an important resource for the people of Northwich, Cheshire, with some 28 km of footpaths, cycleways and canal towpaths.

ADAS's (2016) report for CPRE gives many more examples of improvements to Green Belt land in Northumberland, Yorkshire and the Midlands. Much more could be done with greater vision. Sewage farms in the Green Belt? Well, of course. It surrounds urban areas, which produce lots of sewage. It does not follow that we should build houses in it, but we could, with a bit of ambition, put the sewage farms underground, as they are doing in China (Smart Cities Dive, no date). We could and should improve the Green Belt in all sorts of other ways.

The case is powerfully made by the Chair of the government's Natural Capital Committee, Dieter Helm (2015), in his essay 'In defence of the Green Belt'. Helm points out that the economic case for developing within the Green Belt – that the monetary value of any part of it could be massively increased – applies equally to an asset like St. James's Park in Central London. Building over even a small corner of the park would raise huge sums of money that could be used to do good. However, the same marginal case could be made for the next bit of land and the bit after, until there was no park (or no Green Belt) left. Marginal analysis, he says, should not be applied to the Green Belt as it is a system: 'The Green Belt is not *particular* fields and woodlands. It is these fields and woodlands and so on in *total*' (Helm, 2015, emphases in original).

If one accepts that the Green Belt is a system, not merely a collection of places whose current contribution as Green Belt should be weighed against their potential contribution if they were developed, one needs to ask whether it provides adequate public benefit. Here, I think Dieter Helm is too dismissive of its current environmental and amenity value. However, he is right to point to its potential for increasing natural capital. The government is committed to ensuring that ours will be the first generation to leave the natural environment in a better state than we inherited it. It is hard to see how this aim can be achieved without both protecting and enhancing the Green Belt.

Two immediate opportunities for improvement present themselves. Post-Brexit, the Common Agricultural Policy will need to be replaced.

Agricultural support could be redirected to improve the countryside around towns, from which most people are able to benefit. Second, all parties say that they want to increase tree cover. Why not start with community forests along the inner edge of Green Belts? This would improve natural capital, provide a buffer against development, and please Green Belt critics who are concerned that it is not doing enough for nature or people to justify its existence.

How the Green Belt is being eroded

To give confidence that it is worthwhile improving the Green Belt, people must believe in its permanence. If everyone assumes that it is only a matter of time until development consent is given, no one will invest in its enhancement. Currently, the Green Belt is more respected in politicians' speeches than in reality: when it comes to building in it, ministers look the other way. Research published by CPRE in May 2017 revealed plans to release land sufficient for 425,000 homes from the Green Belt, an increase of 150,000 since the previous survey in March 2016, and that Green Belt boundaries were changing at the fastest rate for over 20 years.[13] Not all the planned homes will be built, but many will be. Moreover, the government will pay at least £2 billion through the New Homes Bonus to support this building boom, in effect giving councils an incentive to set aside the strong Green Belt protections that it says it wants to uphold. The report shows a doubling in the number of planning applications approved year on year for greenfield sites in the Green Belt since the NPPF came into force in 2012, yet only 16% of the homes built are 'affordable'. Most are low-density and high-cost.

If we devoted as much energy to improving the Green Belt as is currently spent trying to build in it, we would have a richer, better-used countryside. We would also have a more constructive debate about the 'very special circumstances' that can justify building in the Green Belt and the 'exceptional circumstances' that can justify redrawing its boundaries. The scale of current development makes a mockery of those planning tests: development in the Green Belt is nothing special, and it is not exceptional for land to be withdrawn from it. Everyone, except it seems those whose duty it is to uphold planning policy, can see this. No wonder countryside campaigners tend to resist even the smallest encroachment.

Redrawing Green Belt boundaries

However, for all that Dieter Helm makes a strong case for holding on to every square inch of the Green Belt, even for increasing it, many in CPRE would be up for a debate on Green Belt boundaries if they did not feel that even talking about change risked the deluge. Yes, the Green Belt is worth fighting for, but it is not holy ground. CPRE does not generally oppose development on brownfield sites within the Green Belt, provided that the developments do not compromise its openness or lead to other problems such as traffic congestion. Beyond that, I have heard three main arguments within CPRE for a debate, if no more, on the role of the Green Belt in the 21st century.

- It is hard to deny that the Green Belt displaces development and development pressure to non-protected land that may be of higher landscape or amenity value. In a perfect system, this land would have better protection. The alternative need not be between building in the Green Belt and the sort of speculative planning applications troubling villages across the country. But we do not have a perfect system, so the choice is often between losing Green Belt or losing other, more precious countryside. For this reason it is worth considering the planning consultancy Urbed's (2014: 2) argument for taking a limited number of 'confident bites' out of the Green Belt.

  They argue that it would sometimes be better to accept a high-quality, well-planned development in a given Green Belt in return for an end to threats to the surrounding countryside and the rest of that Green Belt. A once-in-a-generation settlement of this sort would protect Green Belt and non-Green Belt countryside, while also providing much needed, high-quality development in economically vibrant Green Belt cities. Urbed won the 2014 Wolfson prize for their proposed urban extension to the fictional city of Uxcester. Their itch to turn Oxford into Uxcester, doubling the size of that small and beautiful mediaeval city, is unlikely ever to win CPRE's support. However, their proposal to increase the population of Sheffield by 100,000, partly by developing within the city's Green Belt, won a largely positive response from CPRE South Yorkshire (Urbed, 2015).

- Many Green Belt boundaries were agreed 40 or 50 years ago. No one now remembers why some are tightly drawn and other more loosely. Given the chance, most planners (and CPRE is full of retired planners) could redraw these boundaries in ways that did not compromise the Green Belt's five purposes, but allowed for necessary development.

- In doing so, they might seek to combine the best of Green Belt policy (its robustness) with a 'green wedges' or 'green fingers' approach that brings the countryside into the city. That is how the Sheffield Green Belt works, though most other Green Belts are less successful in connecting town and country. Where the policy is merely one of green wedges without the back-up of an inflexible Green Belt policy, experience suggests that the wedges are relatively easily eroded, which is one reason why CPRE Hampshire and Hampshire County Council now want a Green Belt around Southampton. However, more could be done to use the Green Belt to connect town and country.

These debates take place within CPRE, but conservationists are highly unlikely to invite a public debate or make concessions while the planning system is in such disarray and the Green Belt under such threat. Green Belts only work if they are seen to be permanent, and not up for grabs. However, 'permanent' is used in a curious planner's sense meaning 'open to periodic review'. It is how the reviews are carried out that is important. They should happen no more than once every 15 years and with a very high bar (proof of 'exceptional circumstances') before boundaries can be altered. Boundary reviews should be public and consider the Green Belt as a whole, acknowledging, in Dieter Helm's (2015, emphasis in original) words, that 'it is a *system* and not a set of atomized marginal bits'.

It would be easier to debate the role of the Green Belt if Green Belt policy was respected. However, the fact that it is not means that there is no trust in the system or in the protestations of politicians that they will uphold it. As Rowan Moore (2017) says, at the heart of the debate is a question of trust.

> In theory it should be possible to build on a very small proportion of the nation's green belts in such a way that affordable housing and sustainable communities are created, and more people have more and better access to nature than before. In practice few people trust that this will happen, as the available evidence is that we will get instead a smearing of developers' standard products across the countryside, for sale at inflated prices.

Moore (2017) was writing in praise of a development on previously Green Belt land outside Cambridge: 'If the model can be followed in other green locations across the country we might find a way to create large numbers of decent homes and respect nature at the same time', he says. It is a beguiling thought. However, it is worth noting that the Green Belt release in question was supported by CPRE Cambridgeshire as a once-in-a-generation exercise. Less than 10 years later, developers and politicians are clamouring for more. Those fighting to defend the Oxford Green Belt have taken note. 'Bloody-minded defence' is likely to remain the default position of countryside campaigners until the blanket threat to the Green Belt is lifted.

Notes

[1] See: http://news.sky.com/story/minister-we-must-build-homes-in-countryside-10462567

[2] Department for Communities and Local Government (DCLG) Land use change statistics – live tables 2015 to 2016, Table 350, 2 March 2017, available at:

https://www.gov.uk/government/uploads/system/uploads/attachment_data/file/595736/1516_Land_Use_Change_Statistics_Live_Tables_Feb_revision.xlsx

[3] Shelter submission for the 2014 Wolfson Economics Prize, available at: https://england.shelter.org.uk/__data/assets/pdf_file/0005/941324/SHELTER_WolfsonPrize_WEB.pdf

[4] See: https://www.cpre.org.uk/resources/countryside/tranquil-places/item/download/269

[5] For the debate on how much of England is covered by golf courses, see Shelter's blog on the issue, available at: http://blog.shelter.org.uk/2014/06/hit-a-bunker-how-more-or-less-got-it-wrong-on-the-golf-stat/. As I have discovered in writing this book, most figures on land take are highly contestable.

[6] See: https://www.cpre.org.uk/resources/countryside/tranquil-places/item/download/266

[7] See: https://www.cpre.org.uk/resources/countryside/tranquil-places/item/download/267

[8] With apologies to readers from other parts of the UK. I know that a similar section could be written about any of the home nations, but not by me: it is England I know best.

[9] U.A. Fanthorpe, 'Earthed', available at: www.poetryarchive.org/poem/earthed

[10] Ian Nairn, *Outrage* (London 1955). This was the June 1955 special issue of the *Architectural Review*. The quotations come from the title page of the reprint, published the same year, and from page 365.

[11] See: https://www.visit-dorset.com/explore/thorncombe-p1124493

[12] See: http://londongreenbeltcouncil.org.uk/wp-content/uploads/2016/02/1955-Circular.pdf

[13] 'Green Belt under siege: 2017', available at: https://www.cpre.org.uk/resources/housing-and-planning/green-belts/item/download/5066

FIVE

How the planning system lost its legitimacy, and how to regain it

Introducing the second reading of the Town and Country Planning Bill in January 1947, Lewis Silkin captured the post-war era's high hopes for planning. He half-heartedly demurred from the suggestion that the Bill was 'the most important for a century' ('I should not go as far as that') but said that he was conscious of 'the great responsibility which falls on me in introducing a Bill of this magnitude and historic character'. It is hard to imagine anyone today talking in similar terms about a planning measure, or matching Silkin's stirring peroration:

> When this Bill becomes law, we shall have created an instrument of which we can be justly proud; we shall have begun a new era in the life of this country, an era in which human happiness, beauty, and culture will play a greater part in its social and economic life than they have ever done before. (House of Commons, 29 January 1947)[1]

I do not suggest that everyone was enthused by planning. Decisions on land use can harm some even as they benefit others. The year before, when Silkin went to Stevenage to tell its residents that it was to become a new town, with a tenfold increase in population, he was jeered at a public meeting ("It is no good your jeering: it is going to be done") and the tyres of his ministerial Wolseley were let down. The signs at the local railway station were temporarily changed to 'Silkingrad' (Kynaston, 2007: 161–2).

Yet, Silkin's 1947 speech is a reminder of a time when planning was viewed, in Ellis and Henderson's (2014: 4) words, as 'more than just a way to help you object to your neighbour's conservatory. It was focused not just on where we should live, but on how we should live.' Planning has lost that ambition. It has also lost the muscularity that allowed Silkin and others to establish the new towns. While few would want a return to 'the man in Whitehall knows best' mindset, in its place we have the worst of all worlds: a system that has lost public support but is so weak that it is unable to direct development to the most appropriate places or bring forward a sufficient supply of affordable land for development. The job of planning our future land use has been delegated to hundreds of local authorities with neither the power nor money to deliver.

Planning has become a battleground. The system almost ensures that participants take unreasonable positions. Conservationists and local people take up opposition almost in principle because they have no confidence in what will emerge from the process. On the other side, developers, knowing that they will be opposed, use their legal and financial power to browbeat weak local authorities to get what they want. Local authorities, desperate to meet housing targets, too often accept any old rubbish. Ministers look the other way while ensuring that the Planning Inspectorate gives priority to housing delivery over all the other things that planning is meant to achieve, and everyone complains, even the house builders, agents and lawyers, who make loads of money out of the whole business. It is a mess. Here, in brief, is how it works. Some of the elements of this picture are unpicked later in this chapter.

The planning merry-go-round

Figure 5.1: The planning merry-go-round

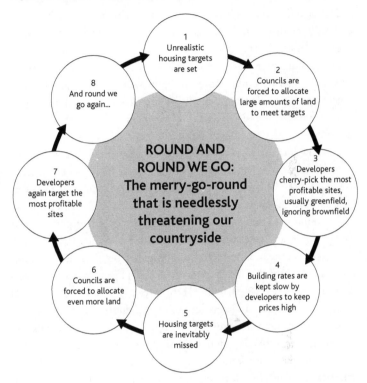

Source: CPRE

Unattainable and often excessive housing targets are set in local plans. The targets take no account of the capacity of the building industry to deliver. Sometimes they assume that more homes will be built year after year than have ever been built, even in boom years. They are based on inconsistent and flawed methodologies, generally developed by companies with a direct financial interest in house building. Local authorities and civil society organisations lack the resources to query the figures. At the time of writing, the government is proposing a single methodology, but this is likely to compound the problem by, in effect, imposing even higher (and still undeliverable) targets on high-demand areas. Furthermore, because planning has become principally a tool for housing delivery, little account is taken of infrastructure pressures or environmental constraints.

So, what happens? Everyone focuses on the targets, not on what realistically can be built. More energy is spent arguing about scary targets than is ever devoted to getting good-quality homes built where they are needed for the people who need them. But the battle over targets is a phoney war because the target is always missed.

The government is understandably concerned about under-delivery and wants a delivery test for local authorities, which will force them to release more land for development if the target is missed. However, local authorities depend on private sector house builders to build on the scale required, and the industry is dominated by a few big firms who have no interest in greatly increasing their output. In July 2017, Shelter estimated that the number of homes completed between 2011/12 and 2015/16 was a third of the number given planning permission between 2010/11 and 2014/15 (Shelter, 2017b). Meanwhile, the pre-tax profits of the top five house builders rose to £3.3 billion in 2016.

Rather than delivering at volume, house builders cherry-pick the easiest, most profitable, greenfield sites. When it is clear that the housing target is not being met, the local authority is required to release more land. If it does not, it is deemed not to have a valid local plan, the presumption in favour of 'sustainable' development kicks in and everywhere is at potential risk of development. If the council does release more land, developers will continue to target the most profitable sites and dribble out supply at a rate that suits their shareholders, rather than public policy. They will also argue the toss about the viability of building affordable homes or doing anything much that could harm their profit margins.

The chances are that the local authority will cave in and drop the standards set out in the local plan. It will also probably give in to speculative proposals for new houses in areas not included in the plan.

If it resists, it risks losing on appeal on the grounds of not having a valid local plan with a five-year land supply. Developers and land-promotion companies, like the notorious Gladman, know this. They game the system, preying on local authorities that cannot prove a five-year supply of deliverable land. If the local authority resists and sticks to its plan, they go to appeal. If they lose, they dust down the proposal and resubmit, with small modifications. It is an unequal war of attrition.

Planning should be more than this. It should be about creating better places. Instead, we have this (un)merry-go-round: a slow, costly, arcane and acrimonious process, a million miles from Lewis Silkin's brave new world.

Need and demand

Local authorities should meet housing need, provided that they can do so sustainably and without eroding protected areas. What does 'need' mean? In the UK context, it should mean more than everyone having a roof over their heads. We should aspire to everyone having a decent home at a price they can afford. Those living in good homes should be careful not to deny the same to others. But for all that we should regard decent housing as a 'good', there are other goods, including a beautiful, productive countryside: a countryside we farm, quarry and use for energy and to mitigate or help us adapt to climate change; which we value for nature and recreation; which helps form our national identity; and where many people live.

I have heard even the most implacable countryside campaigners concede that, if necessary, they would sacrifice some countryside, even protected countryside, to provide homes for those in need. But losing countryside to meet housing need is one thing; losing it to satisfy someone's desire for a bigger or a second home or a lucrative investment is quite another. Housing *need* is not the same as *housing demand*. A word means the thing that it means and not some other thing. So, it is unfortunate that planning policy confuses need and demand. As the Local Government Association's Planning Advisory Service notes: 'The concept of housing need is a keystone of the new planning system, yet it is not defined in either the NPPF [National Planning Policy Framework] or PPG [Planning Practice Guidance].'[2]

When he gave his February 2017 Campaign to Protect Rural England (CPRE) lecture, the then Housing Minister Gavin Barwell acknowledged the distinction between 'genuine "housing need"' and 'aspirational demand': 'I fully accept', he said, 'that we cannot meet the demand of everyone who would like to live in the Cotswolds, the Peak District or the Yorkshire Dales' (Barwell, 2017). That was welcome, but what about those who want to live in the Green Belt in or around Surrey, Oxford, Chester or Leeds? Or in Areas of Outstanding Natural Beauty (AONBs) under increasing threat from high housing targets arising from the confusion between need and demand? Or in other, non-protected areas of countryside? Should we try to meet demand, rather than need, everywhere?

As with so many things in planning, the answer is: 'it depends'. Planning involves judgement. It is a collective exercise in weighing evidence, debating principles and determining the best outcome for a particular area in the context of national guidance. It is not acceptable for local authorities or communities simply to reject the desire of people who are already adequately housed to have a better home. So, in principle, councils should plan to meet demand as well as need, if this can be done sustainably.

Kate Barker (2014: 84) makes a strong ethical case for this approach. She warns that if we cannot satisfy the demand for 'more and bigger dwellings' that grows as income grows:

the better-off will continue to be able to afford the space they would like. The poorer will need larger subsidies.... Those just above the subsidy level will find they have to share more and have smaller dwellings than they would like. An increasing gap will emerge between those who inherit housing wealth and those who do not.... There will be a significant incentive for households to regard housing as an investment.

There is not much to like in that. We have to build more homes, and not only for those in need.

However, that does not mean that the aim of planning should be to satisfy all housing demand. Demand, our desires as individuals and consumers, should not always hold sway. We are citizens as well as 'market actors', and our first-order desires as consumers may clash with our deeper wishes concerning the sort of country that we want to live in. The housing market indicates people's personal preferences for the housing they want, but it is planning that seeks to capture the public interest, our wishes as citizens. I might desire a big house in spacious grounds for myself, but I do not want everyone else to be able to exercise their desires because I also value the countryside and do not want to see it eaten up. This is one reason we have a democratic planning system and a policy of urban containment: to assert the public interest in the use of land against our desires as individuals.

We should be worried that some councils are doing more to meet demand than need. In London, for instance, local authorities can meet their housing targets by building large numbers of luxury flats. This is good for foreign investors but bad for neighbourhoods and, even with some cross-subsidy for affordable housing, does little for those in housing need. It is forecast that over the next five years there will be an over-provision of the most expensive housing in London (in anticipation of international demand) and an under-provision of the most affordable (Walker, 2017: 14).

A second, practical objection to the idea that we should aim to meet housing demand is that it is based on what individuals, households and investors are able and willing to pay, which is potentially limitless. Indeed, it really does seem limitless today in London, where property is such an attractive investment for the global mega-rich.

Aspirational growth

As well as planning to meet need and demand, some councils set ambitious targets for economic growth, which, in turn, inflate housing targets. There are many examples; here are a few:

- Political and business leaders in Oxfordshire, still the most rural county in the South-East, want to generate 85,000 new jobs, a major reason why its planning authorities must plan for 100,000 new homes. House building will be needed across the county on a scale never seen before, even in boom years. Neither the growth aspirations nor the housing targets have been downgraded or even re-evaluated following the European Union (EU) referendum. Whatever the effect that one thinks Brexit will have on economic and population growth, it is surely reasonable to assume that it will have some impact.

- The Leeds Core Strategy, adopted in November 2014, set a housing requirement of 4,375 homes a year for the 16-year duration of the plan. This was over 1,300 more homes a year than the government's household projections suggested were needed, but was justified by the council on the basis of its aspirations for employment growth. Predictably, it was not possible to establish a five-year land supply for housing growth on this scale. In 2017, the local authority agreed to set a new target. However, the process takes at least a year, and in the meantime, Leeds lacks a valid local plan and is subject to planning by appeal under the presumption in favour of sustainable development (Walker, 2017: 24).

- In September 2016, the joint core strategy for Cheltenham, Gloucester and Tewksbury assumed annual economic growth of 4.6% for the duration of the plan. This was the aspirational target of the Local Enterprise Partnership (LEP). It will not be achieved. Every LEP wants its area to grow above average and local authorities have to plan houses to accommodate the workers who will (it is hoped) deliver this growth.

It is fine for a local authority to plan for growth, but under the current system, even if the growth fails to materialise, it is obliged to meet the housing targets that were predicated on that growth. A local authority planning for growth must meet the viability and deliverability tests set out in the NPPF (paragraphs 47 and 173) or it will be deemed not to have a valid plan (DCLG, 2012). Urbed's bold plan to expand

Sheffield, mentioned in Chapter Four, is incompatible with the current system, as they acknowledge:

> Much of the 70,000 home capacity of the urban area cannot be measured to the satisfaction of a planning inspector and in any case would fail the deliverability test. If Sheffield were therefore to go with the ambitious growth figures that we suggest they could find themselves forced to make more greenfield allocations. The best way to avoid this is to downplay the city's growth figures. (Urbed, 2015: 2)

In other words, if Sheffield went for growth, the developers would not build on the brownfield sites allocated, nor would they deliver the sort of high-quality homes and ambitious place-making that Urbed propose. Instead, they would plead non-viability and get permission for greenfield development. This makes ambitious plan-making impossible. It would surely be better to *require* local authorities to meet housing need but *allow* them to set aspirational plans for growth without putting them at risk of not having a valid plan if they failed to deliver that growth.

In reality, many local authorities are basing their housing numbers on ambitious plans for employment growth, but without Urbed's commitment to quality and urbanism. For many CPRE branches, it is these 'boosterist' economic growth policies – unrealistic and undeliverable housing targets to meet unrealistic and undeliverable employment targets – that lie at the root of the planning system's dysfunction. Housing targets can be twice what would be needed to address demographic change. This also has a bearing on the issue of population because it is only through immigration that many local authorities could possibly create a workforce to support their growth ambitions. The need for more house building is often blamed on immigration, but immigration is necessary to meet the economic ambitions that drive the housing targets.

Objectively Assessed Need

Too often, local authorities and planning inspectors not only mix up need, demand and aspirations for economic growth in their calculation of the Objectively Assessed Need (OAN) for new housing, but also treat OAN as a target, rather than as one piece of evidence (albeit an important one) to help inform a local plan. The NPPF gives many examples of when OAN does not have to be met, or at least where judgement should be exercised, but these are ignored.[3] Then, as we have seen, the target is missed, the local authority is deemed not to have a valid plan, the presumption in favour of sustainable development kicks in and there is a development free-for-all. Big homes are built in the countryside for those who can afford them; those in housing need remain in need.

One of the problems is that the whole business of calculating housing targets has grown too complicated. There is a good deal of money to be made by developers and a complicated system suits big firms who can afford to navigate it. The system is a long way from what the government intended when it introduced the NPPF in 2012. In his foreword to the NPPF, Planning Minister Greg Clark said that people had been put off getting involved in shaping the places they lived:

> because planning policy itself has become so elaborate and forbidding – the preserve of specialists, rather than people in communities. This National Planning Policy Framework changes that. By replacing over a thousand pages of national policy with around fifty, written simply and clearly, we are allowing people and communities back into planning. (DCLG, 2012: ii)

It has not worked out that way. Local plan-making has become so complicated and disempowering that CPRE is one of the last civic or environmental bodies still seriously engaged. This is seen most starkly in examinations into local plans. Here, it is not unknown for a solitary volunteer from CPRE to face a dozen barristers from the development industry. The inquiry becomes largely an argument between developers (to take one example, in West Oxfordshire in 2015, 24 builders or landowners were represented, three environmental or civic groups, and three local authorities). No wonder people grow cynical.

So, how should we set targets for new housing (net additions to the stock, not just new build)?

- OAN should be calculated according to a transparent methodology that distinguishes between need, demand and aspirational growth targets.
- The housing target should be informed by OAN, but might be lower if this was necessary to protect Green Belt and other designated land. A local authority going for growth might want to exceed OAN, but would not be forced to release more greenfield land or abandon its plan if the growth failed to materialise.
- The public sector should ensure that enough affordable homes are built, and work to support the private sector's delivery of the market housing for which there is demand.
- Local planning should take place in the context of a national spatial plan that seeks to direct economic development to parts of the country most in need, rather than simply stoking growth in the crowded South-East.

Under any system, including the current one, local authorities should not just draw up a plan and wait for developers to deliver it, but should actively promote new housing. Those with Green Belt or AONB land should work extra hard to bring forward brownfield land for development.

Brownfield first

This does not just mean identifying old factory sites or disused public land; it also means carrying out full urban capacity studies to identify potential sites, including small sites. It means being imaginative about the redevelopment potential of town centres, which waste space on surface car parks and single-story shopping centres. I am fully behind those who want to protect the Green Belt around Guildford in Surrey, for instance, but many more people could live in Guildford town centre, which could be improved by careful densification. At present, it wastes space.

In 2014, CPRE's crowd-sourcing campaign, #wasteofspace, asked the public to identify empty buildings or disused brownfield land that might be suitable for development. The response suggests that there is considerable untapped housing potential in towns and cities. This was clearly demonstrated by the University of the West of England research into the availability of brownfield land, *From wasted space to living spaces* (Sinnett et al, 2014), which established that there was enough suitable brownfield land in England for at least 976,000 homes. It showed how the stock of brownfield land is replenished more quickly than it is used: previously developed land is a stream, not a reservoir. Finally, it showed that around half the potential for new homes on brownfield land was in London and the South-East (Sinnett et al, 2014).

When the Coalition came to power in 2010, it abolished the brownfield-first presumption in planning, together with the target of building homes at densities of 30–50 dwellings per hectare. Urban regeneration and the idea of an urban renaissance were associated with New Labour and, in particular, John Prescott, a Conservative bogeyman. The free-market think tanks and the Home Builders Federation wanted more freedom, and the government gave it to them. The promise was increased output, but this has not been delivered. Now, the government has signalled a greater willingness to intervene in the housing market. It should seize the opportunity to reboot the urban agenda and promote compact, low-carbon developments.

Can planning regain its legitimacy?

If planning has a crisis of legitimacy, so does the political system within which it sits. We seem to have lost faith in politics itself – Bernard Crick's 'great and civilising human activity'. This is bad news for planning, which is an intrinsically political business. Its job of mediating between often conflicting sectional interests in the wider public interest involves controversy, argument and compromise. It elevates the public interest over individual desires, which goes against the grain of our individualist, consumerist age. As Professor Gerry Stoker (quoted in Flinders, 2012: 84) puts it:

> the discourse and practice of collective decision-making sits very uncomfortably alongside the discourse and practice of individual choice, self-expression and market-based fulfilment of needs and wants … so it turns out that a propensity to disappoint is an inherent feature of governance even in democratic societies.

One could say the same of planning, though 'a propensity to disappoint' is unlikely to become the strapline of any planning authority. When decisions are taken on land use, some people are bound to be disappointed. But planning at least provides a structure for those decisions, and allows for public influence. It explicitly seeks to serve the public interest, a noble aim. If planning has a propensity to disappoint, non-planning would provide greater disappointment to more people.

If the public is losing belief in planning, the solution is not to depoliticise it by making it more responsive to market signals or putting 'experts' in charge. You can no more take politics out of planning than you can make politics non-political. Part of the solution is to engage more people and get their buy-in. Neighbourhood planning is a good way of doing this, provided that neighbourhood plans are respected. However, the planning system must also show that it can deliver.

It may be an uphill task to get people to believe in planning while there is such scepticism about politics, but it would be considerably easier if the system ensured sufficient development in the places agreed in the plan while also managing, as Silkin intended, 'to safeguard the beauty of the countryside and coast-line'.[4] While there is insufficient development overall but too much happening in an unplanned way, it will be hard to restore a belief in planning.

Vignette

On 21 September 2017, the front-page headline of the Maidstone edition of the *Kent Messenger* was: 'More, more, more: thousands of extra homes could be forced on borough.' What is going on here? We need to build more houses, so why the outrage? Was this just another appeal to Nimbys from a newspaper in the shires?

I think it is a bit more complicated than that and that Maidstone's case (I apologise for another Kentish example) is typical of what is going wrong with our housing and planning system. The story followed the Communities Secretary's proposal that where average house prices are more than four times average salaries, housing targets should increase. The paper noted: 'This weekend new three-bedroom terraces, just a stone's throw from Tovil tip, will go on the market priced from £312,500 – more than 12-and-a-half times the average salary.' Maidstone, it said, would have to increase its housing target from 17,660 new homes by 2031 to 'an astonishing' 24,720.

Panicked by the suggestion that it would have to raise its target, the council postponed the adoption of its local plan, 11 years in the making. According to Helen Grant MP, 'Maidstone is bursting at the seams and the South East is crippled by a lack of infrastructure, congestion and air pollution. More housing is only making this worse and should be concentrated in other areas' (*Kent Messenger*, 2017).

My concern here is not specifically with Maidstone. You can read similar stories in local newspapers across the country. But it is worth noting two things. First, without major changes to national policy, the housing target will not be reached. There are not the builders to build 17,660 homes in Maidstone, let alone 24,720. These are fantasy targets. If homes were built on this scale under the current system, they would be poor-quality, very few would be affordable and they would add to Maidstone's daily traffic gridlock. Second, the council is out of its depth. I say this without any particular knowledge of Maidstone Borough Council. I could be more authoritatively rude about other councils. However, I know Maidstone reasonably well and I do not see how even 10,000 extra homes can be provided without much greater powers for local authorities both to build council homes and to assemble land, capture its value and use that value to invest in infrastructure.

Those attacking Nimbys in Maidstone and elsewhere should ask themselves what it will take to persuade reasonable people to accept house building on this scale. People would need to feel that the new homes would actually improve the area and help those in need rather than investors and the better off, and that genuine efforts were being made to maximise the potential of brownfield sites and to rebalance growth across the country. Getting people behind large-scale house building means moving beyond the tired charade of giving local authorities ambitious targets without ensuring that they have the powers and skills to meet them. We know where that ends: too much countryside lost; too few homes built.

Conclusion

Chapter Six summarises some of the solutions to the housing crisis set out so far, and proposes some new ones. If acted on, they would help to restore the legitimacy of the planning system. This matters because tackling the housing crisis is a big task and is made much harder if those most affected (and therefore most likely to protest) have no confidence in how decisions are made.

Notes

[1] *Hansard* (1947) HC vol 432, cols 947, 987.

[2] Objectively Assessed Need and Housing Targets, Planning Advisory Service (PAS), June 2015, p 41, para A1. For the confusion between need and demand, see paragraphs 50 and 159 of the NPPF and paragraph 003 of the PPG on housing and economic development needs assessment, headed 'What is the definition of need?' This states: 'Need for housing in the context of the guidance refers to the scale and mix of housing and the range of tenures that is likely to be needed in the housing market area over the plan period – and should cater for the housing demand of the area and identify the scale of housing supply necessary to meet that demand.'

[3] Paragraph 14 of the NPPF states: 'Local Plans should meet objectively assessed needs ... unless: any adverse impacts of doing so would significantly and demonstrably outweigh the benefits, when assessed against the policies in this Framework taken as a whole; or specific policies in this Framework indicate development should be restricted.' Footnote 9 gives examples of such policies, including those 'relating to sites protected under the Birds and Habitats Directives ... and/or designated as Sites of Special Scientific Interest; land designated as Green Belt, Local Green Space, an Area of Outstanding Natural Beauty, Heritage Coast or within a National Park (or the Broads Authority); designated heritage assets; and locations at risk of flooding or coastal erosion' (DCLG, 2012).

[4] *Hansard* (1947) HC vol 432, col 948.

SIX

Solutions

If we had a planning system we could trust to define growth needs in credible ways and to defend core assets in the long term. *If* we combined that with processes for land assembly and for the public 'capture' of land values that would make the plans deliverable. *If* we had a development industry that produced quality, funded for the long-term with 'patient capital', private and public. *If* we at CPRE [Campaign to Protect Rural England] evolved our position on how Town & Country can be reconciled to meet both development needs and the protection of landscape, the environment and country life.... *Then* we might be able to engage in the creative way our founders did.

Until then, it seems we have to simply keep on saying 'not an inch of the Green Belt, development must be predominantly brownfield', and so on. Because any other posture takes too many risks with our core values. (Crookston, 2016)

Introduction

After the 2017 Housing White Paper was published, Housing Minister Gavin Barwell went around the country saying, 'there's no silver bullet solution. If there was, one of my predecessors would have found it' (Barwell, 2017). He was teased for saying this in countless interviews, but he was right. There rarely are 'silver bullets' in politics, and there are complex and deep-seated reasons why we have failed for many years to build enough new homes of the right sort.

- Economically, a good deal of national and personal wealth is tied up in property. Politicians tread carefully.
- Culturally, land in our small, beautiful and highly populated country has peculiar significance. There is broad national agreement that we should take great care where we build. When politicians or developers ignore this sentiment, they are fiercely resisted. Planning restrictions are an expression of the national will. Weakening planning laws will not stop communities fighting for places they care about.
- Politically, faith in the market and hostility to council housing have been core to post-1979 Conservatism, but the Thatcherite housing legacy is now in tatters. Conservatives must look beyond mythology and ideology to the evidence, and countenance solutions that have been taboo since Mrs Thatcher's time.
- Who is going to build the homes we need? There are too few firms able or willing to do so. The big builders who dominate the market are more effective at trading and banking land than building houses. The market needs many more players, including a greater role for the public sector.
- Land is too expensive. Releasing much more will not, in itself, make it significantly cheaper as land and houses are a magnet for investment. Will any government dare look hard at how we tax land, property and inheritance?
- Local government is too weak. We have a plan-led system but local government in England has been progressively weakened for

decades. Too many local authorities seem incapable of articulating a vision for their area, let alone delivering it. The exception is government in London and other new mayoral authorities: they provide hope of a local government renaissance.

• Where should we build? England lacks any sort of national spatial plan and the assumption underlying policy is that economic wealth should continue to flow to the regions that have the severest housing pressures and the most active civic groups resisting new development.

• Our housing crisis is intimately tied up with wealth inequality, one that has a generational as well as class and spatial dimension. This is recognised across the political parties; the work of the centrist Resolution Foundation, chaired by a Conservative peer, has been particularly influential.

It may be unhelpful to start a chapter entitled 'solutions' with a long list of problems, but many of our recent policy failures were hatched, as it were, in laboratory conditions. Theoretical solutions to particular aspects of the housing crisis are easy to come by, but this is a multilayered problem.

It is also a political problem. Any solutions have to be politically saleable. Given the nature of the problem we face ('I wouldn't start from here …'), this will require strong leadership from a united government prepared to take difficult decisions. As the Great Brexit Adventure swallows political energy and (in the view of most economists) national wealth, it will be hard for any government to make housing the priority that it needs to be. But it is equally hard to see the housing crisis being resolved unless it is. We know the result of partial measures and stop–start policies: too few homes built, too many people in housing need, too much countryside lost.

Shaping town and country

The thesis of this book (and of Martin Crookston's CPRE paper quoted in the epigraph to this chapter) is that people who currently oppose housing development can be persuaded to support it if there are serious changes to policy. Any successful effort to win trust must start with a new national conversation on housing and planning. This may sound lame but it is hard to exaggerate the sense of disillusion bordering on despair now felt in the shires by those active in local planning. Many CPRE campaigners have spent years working in planning, either as volunteers or professionals. They do not expect always to win, but they now feel both that the odds are stacked against them and that those in authority are in denial about the failures of the system. When politicians insist that the countryside is safe with them, in spite of all evidence to the contrary, it is hard to have an honest conversation.

But if the authorities were serious about creating a better system, it would be incumbent on CPRE activists to help plan for housing growth. This was the gist of a draft statement, 'Shaping town and country', drawn up by CPRE and Urbed in 2015. We hoped to encourage a less polarised national debate on housing numbers, urban growth and the Green Belt. The intention was to get support from CPRE's branches and members, then invite a wide range of other organisations to sign up to the principles in the statement. In the event, the statement was not made public and it remains unpublished. Local CPRE activists we consulted were unenthusiastic. Their message was: 'anyone can think of a better way of doing things, but the government won't listen and the countryside is under attack. We can't afford distractions.' There was also a sense that even to talk about the Green Belt risked weakening its protection. This was understandable but, in retrospect, I regret not pushing on with the initiative.

The draft statement set out the need to plan for substantially more housing, particularly affordable housing, and also to provide land for employment, transport and services.

Currently, we do this badly. We fail to provide enough homes and those that we do build are often unaffordable and poorly served by infrastructure. Yet very little of the value generated by building this new housing is spent on infrastructure, the costs of which instead fall on the public purse. The planning system has become adversarial and procedural. We have lost sight of its role in positively shaping the location and type of new development and therefore the shape of our towns and cities, and their relationship to the surrounding countryside.

Because of this many people have lost faith in the ability of the development industry and the planning system to produce places, homes and jobs in the right locations and of the right quality.

The paper proposed six principles for a better system:

1. A brownfield target: 'The first priority should always be to build within existing urban areas', with a national target of at least 60% of new housing on brownfield land and a requirement on local authorities to explore fully the capacity of their urban areas before considering greenfield land release.
2. Plan positively for greenfield development: up to 40% of housing nationally will be built outside urban areas, and we should plan it well. Approval of greenfield development should be subject to three conditions: land should only be allocated for development following a review of its landscape, heritage and ecological, archaeological or agricultural value, and taking account of existing designations; it should only be allocated where it can be served by public transport and sustainable infrastructure, and linked to existing communities and employment opportunities; if a Green Belt is reviewed, 'it must be reviewed as a whole and in relation to all of its purposes, not chipped away site-by-site in order to meet short term requirements. Any Green Belt release will still require exceptional circumstances to be demonstrated'.
3. 'Local planning authorities should take the lead in agreeing the location and scale of development.' They should consider designating 'growth areas' if land with potential for housing development is not being brought forward by the market. 'Growth area' status would bring additional planning and land acquisition powers.
4. Development should be sustainable and well designed, with access to public transport and a range of facilities. It 'should be planned to

enhance the surrounding countryside', not 'something we need to screen from view'. The development process should encourage a greater number of players: not only large house builders, but small builders, local authorities, housing associations, self-builders and custom builders.

5. Land assembly: new mechanisms should be introduced to coordinate and plan large-scale development and create local institutions that can build long-term trust in the consistency and predictability of planning decisions. 'These mechanisms should allow land required in the public interest to be easily and swiftly acquired.'

6. Land value capture: 'Mechanisms are needed to capture part of the economic value created by development in the public interest'. A proportion of the value created when land is developed should be used to meet the infrastructure needs generated by that development. 'Currently this happens very inefficiently, if at all.' The statement suggested (questionably) that with a mechanism for land value capture, large-scale housing developments would not need public subsidy. It did, however, assume an active role for the public sector, including in unlocking private finance by offering long-term guarantees.

Hardly any of this is happening:

- We do not have a brownfield-first policy. Vast areas of suitable brownfield land remain untapped, enough for at least a million new homes, and the stock of brownfield land continues to grow faster than it is developed. There is also scope to revive high streets and sensitively densify urban and suburban areas. Meanwhile, over 50% of new houses are now built on greenfield land. We build fewer homes than 10 years ago, but they take up nearly twice as much greenfield land.

- We do not plan positively for development outside urban areas. There is usually total resistance to greenfield development when it is first proposed but relatively little effort to improve its quality once it has been pushed through planning. Such effort as there is rarely feels successful, which helps explain why development proposals are so strongly resisted in the first place. The conditions proposed in the draft CPRE-Urbed joint statement would certainly improve the greenfield development that will inevitably take place.

- Land is not developed because it is in the best possible location; it is developed because it suits the landowner and the developer. Ribbon development, which CPRE thought it had seen off 70 years ago, has now returned, with homes and businesses strung along supposedly strategic corridors across the country. This builds in car dependency (Sloman et al, 2017: 70, 128).
- Green Belts are not reviewed as a whole: they are chipped away at site by site, and it is far from exceptional for 'exceptional circumstances' to be invoked.
- Local authorities are not strong planners and place makers. Most are caught between powerful developers and their angry opponents, lacking the power and confidence to assemble land and plan high-quality development. Yet, if towns and cities are to thrive, they need strong civic leadership. Developers cannot be made responsible for the quality of their developments. Many have only a short-term interest in it. Some would rather trade land than build on it. To quote Wulf Daseking, Director of City Planning in Freiburg, 'the city that did it all': 'Don't let the developers near. They won't develop' (Hall, 2014: 272).
- Very few developments enhance the surrounding countryside: it hardly seems a consideration. Too many really do have to be screened from view.
- The big builders control the rate of supply.
- There is no adequate system of land value capture.

It is a mess. A new system that followed the principles set out in the CPRE/Urbed draft statement would go a long way to improving the quality of development and overcoming resistance to house building.

What else should we do, or at least consider?

Diversify supply

Local authorities should be allowed to borrow to build (see Chapter One) and the government should increase its funding for housing associations. Rural areas, in particular, need social housing that is affordable in perpetuity. The government should redouble its efforts to support small builders and custom building.

Taxation and controlling property prices

Stable or gently falling house prices should be an aim of policy. The government should consult on a range of potential changes to taxation, including: a land value tax; Council Tax revaluation and the introduction of new bands; extending capital gains tax to primary properties, with the charge rolled over a lifetime; and lowering the threshold of inheritance tax (Barker, 2014: 56–81). VAT on refurbishments and greenfield development should be equalised. For years, governments have said that they cannot do this because of European Union (EU) rules. Soon, if Brexit goes ahead as planned, they will be able to.

Raise standards

Local authorities in theory have the power to turn down poor quality developments; the government and the Planning Inspectorate should encourage them to use it. The Commission on Architecture and the Built Environment (CABE) should be brought back, or some other body to encourage quality design and place making created. If government schemes such as the New Homes Bonus and Help to Buy must continue, payments should be restricted to brownfield developments or developments of the very highest quality on greenfield land.

Green the Green Belt

The Green Belt is worth protecting whether or not it is green. But it is easier to defend if it serves a strong recreational and environmental purpose. We should devote part of a new post-Common Agricultural Policy land support policy to improving the quality of countryside closest to where the mass of the population lives, notably, the Green Belt.

Plan strategically

I am reluctant to suggest radical planning reform as this can slow down development for several years while everyone gets used to the new system. However, the current system is bust. In its operation, if not in theory, it elevates housing targets above all other considerations without giving local authorities the means to achieve them. There are big loopholes that encourage unscrupulous developers and land promoters to game the system. Planning should be about place making, sustainable transport, enhancing nature, tackling climate change and many other good things. The current system generally fails to deliver these things. It even fails in its principal aim: delivering high numbers of new homes. It needs reform.

At the same time, local government must be strengthened and given the resources to plan positively. The duty on local authorities to cooperate with their neighbours has not been a success. We need some sort of strategic planning, along the lines of the old county structure plans, or even regional planning.

Below the level of local (or county) planning, neighbourhood planning should be encouraged and strengthened. It is the best way to engage large numbers of people in the planning process. However, there is also a role for national planning: a national land-use strategy and, sitting alongside it, a national spatial plan. There is vast potential for regenerating towns and cities, including in the rich South-East. There is still a good deal of untapped potential even in London. But there may also be a case for new settlements and large-scale urban extensions. They could house large numbers of people sustainably and, with the right policy framework, be built to exemplary standards of design and sustainability. They would certainly be much preferable to the sort of 'plonking' of new estates in the countryside by towns and villages that we now see. The process of developing a thorough national spatial plan would help us determine the need for new settlements, and where they should go.

New civic house building

While I was writing this book, Shelter came out with their own proposals for 'rediscovering our tradition of building beautiful and affordable homes' (Jefferys and Lloyd, 2017). They call this plan 'new civic house building' and it is hard to fault. Its basis is the insistence (as set out in the Urbed/CPRE draft statement and in Chapter One of this book) that the price paid for land should be low enough to allow for high-quality developments in line with local plans (Jefferys and Lloyd, 2017: 47). This would allow beautiful places to be built for the long term, following a unified master plan.

After giving a number of historical and contemporary examples of quality development, the authors note that these exemplar schemes are the exception, not the rule: 'Far more often, the land market and planning system between them incentivise speculative development at the expense of quality and local needs' (Jefferys and Lloyd, 2017: 82). New civic house building requires 'a strong intervention in the land market' (Jefferys and Lloyd, 2017: 86) to acquire land at low cost. Landowners would have the option of investing their land as equity into a development partnership, giving a long-term return: what is proposed is certainly less hostile to landowner interests than the policy supported by Churchill during the war.

What is most valuable about the new civic house-building model is the breadth of its ambition. It argues persuasively that we can build large numbers of beautiful, sustainable, affordable homes with a large degree of public consent. Most of these large-scale developments will be extensions to existing settlements, or on large brownfield sites.

Some, inevitably, will be on greenfield sites, but that is nothing new: it is happening all over the country now, but without the quality or affordability. Other forms of house building would continue but the hope is that the 'new model' developments will raise standards and ambition.

New civic housebuilding is a tonic because its optimistic vision contrasts so markedly with the reality of much of the development we see today and with the tired, zombie arguments still peddled every day that what we need to do to get more homes built is take on the Nimbys and have (another) terrific scrap over the Green Belt.

Meanwhile, the government, overwhelmed both by Brexit and the aftermath of the Grenfell fire, seems out of ideas. But we need new ideas: those that have shaped policy over the last decade have been markedly unsuccessful. There is a powerful alliance to be forged between those whose primary concern is to build more homes in order to combat social injustice, and those who get out of bed each morning ready to fight for the countryside and the wider environment. Their causes are compatible, even complementary. We really can build the houses the country needs while safeguarding our precious, beautiful countryside.

Afterword

In January 2018, the Department for Communities and Local Government (DCLG) was renamed the Ministry of *Housing*, Communities and Local Government in order to reflect the government's 'renewed focus' on house building.[1] Symbolism can be important and one of the arguments in this book is that if ministers really want to get houses built, they have the power to make it happen. It is good that they are signalling that they want to do so. However, I also argue that obsessing about numbers alone is a bad mistake. The country will not get the new houses it needs by privileging numbers over everything else.

Another argument in the book is that the countryside matters. As well as a housing crisis, we have a host of related rural and environmental woes: loss and erosion of landscapes; more species declining than thriving; the suburbanisation of villages and market towns; unequal and acrimonious battles over planning; and climate change. We need to think hard about the location of new homes, and build them in ways that foster nature[2] and help address climate change.

I see no sign that the government is geared to tackle house building with the sharp focus of the post-war governments, let alone address housing in the round. The Prime Minister says she is taking "personal charge"[3] of the government's strategy on house building, but this is implausible given the shadow cast by Brexit. There is precious little space in government ('bandwidth' in the cliché of the day) to focus on anything other than Brexit.

This puts a greater responsibility on local authorities to deliver new housing. A December 2017 report from the National Planning Forum and the Royal Town Planning Institute (RTPI) suggests they are starting to do so. Sixty-five percent of local authorities in England are directly engaged in housing delivery, with 30 local housing companies set up in 2017 alone. The report concludes that there is 'a growing appetite and capacity in local authorities to return to or increase their roles in providing housing as a core function'. They 'are well placed to scale up their delivery of housing, if certain barriers can be addressed' (Morphet and Clifford, 2017: 4).

One frustration for local authorities is the reluctance of developers to build even when they have planning permission. 'Local authorities have learned that there is no obligation on any developer or land agent to build any housing with planning permission; rather their obligation is to shareholders' (Morphet and Clifford, 2017: 4). In responses, councils of all political complexions are building housing themselves, and doing so more quickly than the private sector builders and often on the sort of small or difficult sites shunned by private companies.

Localism is delivering, but the government needs to move on more decisively from Mrs Thatcher's war on local democracy. If councils had greater powers, both to borrow and to resist unacceptable practices by developers and land speculators, they could achieve much more.

Of course, a major role for central government remains. In this Afterword I would just emphasise one area of policy that received relatively perfunctory treatment earlier: the contribution of house building to climate change or (ideally) climate change mitigation. It is ludicrous that we are building houses today that will need retrofitting in a few years' time to reduce fuel costs and increase flood resilience. A serious push to ensure that all new homes are zero carbon will both save consumers money and contribute to meeting the UK's carbon reduction targets. The zero carbon homes target was dropped ostensibly because it was thought that it would make house building more expensive. But experience in other sectors shows that costs can tumble when government sets a clear policy and funding framework.

Five years ago, offshore wind power cost nearly four times more than gas. By 2017, offshore wind cost less than the energy from new gas power plants. This was the direct result of an industrial strategy that committed to deploying offshore wind at scale, subject to a review clause if industry did not cut costs. This 'commit and review' pact was first advanced by Green Alliance in 2014.[4] A similar challenge should now be made to the house building industry. Costs are likely to plummet – but even if they do not, it is worth investing in zero carbon homes. On average, a zero carbon home currently costs around £3,150 more than the average new home, a sum that is paid off by savings on energy bills after around six years (McNamee et al, 2017). Innovation is bound to bring costs down.

A focus on energy efficient housing should extend to the existing housing stock. The government's Clean Growth Strategy aims to retrofit all existing homes to EPC (energy performance certificate) Band C by 2035, but has no strategy for getting there. Since the Grenfell Fire, DCLG (now the MHCLG) has seemed incapable of moving forward the energy efficiency agenda, with the consequence that the country as a whole is set to miss its climate change targets.

A concerted push to make existing homes energy efficient would have significant social, economic and environmental benefits. Modelling by Verco and Cambridge Econometrics suggests that a major retrofit programme would cuts gas imports by a quarter and raise GDP by 0.6% by 2030, and significantly reduce bills, not least for people on low incomes or living in the countryside (see Chapter 3).[5]

Upfront costs would be significant, both for the government and the private sector, and the government is terrified of anything that could be used as an excuse for not building houses or which smacks of economic profligacy. But the investment would quickly pay for itself. Alongside its 'renewed focus' on house building, the government should give a much higher priority to improving the energy efficiency both of new houses and the existing stock – to making sure our homes are fit for the future.

Notes

[1] See: www.insidehousing.co.uk/news/reshuffle-dclg-renamed-ministry-of-housing-communities-and-local-government-53794

[2] See 'Homes for people and wildlife – How to build housing in a nature-friendly way', The Wildlife Trusts, see: www.wildlifetrusts.org/news/2018/01/11/new-guidelines-call-homes-people-and-wildlife

[3] See: www.gov.uk/government/news/pm-we-must-get-back-to-building-the-homes-this-country-needs

[4] Spencer, M., Andrews Tipper, W. and Coats, E. (2014) 'UK offshore wind in the 2020s: creating the conditions for cost effective decarbonisation', Green Alliance. I am grateful to Dustin Benton for this suggestion.

[5] Washan, P., Stenning, J. and Goodman, M. (2014) 'Building the future: the economic and fiscal impacts of making homes energy efficient'. Available at: www.energybillrevolution.org/wp-content/uploads/2014/10/Building-the-Future-The-Economic-and-Fiscal-impacts-of-making-homes-energy-efficient.pdf

References

Abercrombie, P. (1926) *The preservation of rural England*, Liverpool and London: University Press of Liverpool and Hodder and Stoughton.

ADAS (2016) *Nature conservation and recreational opportunities in the Green Belt*, London: CPRE.

Addison, P. (1982 [1977]) *The road to 1945*, London: Quartet.

Airports Commission (2015) *Final report*, London: Airports Commission. Available at: https://www.gov.uk/government/uploads/system/uploads/attachment_data/file/440316/airports-commission-final-report.pdf

Bacon, R. (2017) 'Transforming how we do housing', in R. Pow and M. Holmes (eds) *Thinking differently about our environment: A holistic approach to policy*, London: Conservative Environment Network (CEN).

Banks, C. (2017) 'Time to look again at viability?', Shelter Blog, 3 February. Available at: http://blog.shelter.org.uk/2017/02/time-to-look-again-at-viability/

Barker, K. (2004) *Review of housing supply – Delivering stability: Securing our future housing needs*, London: HMSO.

Barker, K. (2006) *Barker review of land use planning*, London: TSO.

Barker, K. (2014) *Housing: Where's the plan?*, London: London Publishing Partnership.

Barwell, G. (2017) 'CPRE annual lecture'. Available at: https://www.gov.uk/government/speeches/cpre-annual-lecture

Beckett, A. (2016) 'Is Britain full? Home truths about the population panic', *The Guardian*, 9 February. Available at: https://www.theguardian.com/world/2016/feb/09/is-britain-full-home-truths-about-population-panic

Bennet, A. (2011) 'Baffled at a bookcase', *London Review of Books*, 28 July, 33(15): 3–7.

Benson, R. (2006) *The farm*, London: Penguin.

Bentley, D. (2017) *The land question*, London: Civitas.

Bibby, P. and Brindley, P. (2013) 'The 2011 rural–urban classification for small area geographies: a user guide and frequently asked questions (v1.0)', ONS.

Boles, N. (2010) *Which way's up?*, London: Biteback.

Bowie, D. (2017) *Radical solutions to the housing supply crisis*, Bristol: The Policy Press.

Bryson, B. (2000) *Introduction to the English landscape*, London: Profile.

Bryson, B. (2015) *The road to little dribbling*, London: Doubleday.

Burroughs, L. (2015a) *Getting houses built*, London: CPRE.

Burroughs, L. (2015b) *A living countryside*, London: CPRE.

Callcutt Review (2007) *The Callcutt review of housing delivery*, London: HMSO.

Churchill, W. (1945) *The dawn of liberation*, London: Cassell.

Clifford, S. and King, A. (2006) *England in particular*, London: Hodder and Stoughton.

CPRE (1926) 'The aims and objects of the Council', CPRE, December, MERL (Museum of English Life): SR CPRE/D/1/2.

CPRE (1928) 'CPRE Annual Report – 1928', CPRE, MERL, University of Reading (SR CPRE B/1/2).

CPRE (1937) 'CPRE Monthly Report – May 1937'. MERL (SR CPRE B/2/11).

CPRE (1986) 'David Puttnam correspondence Feb-Jul 1986'. MERL (Box 9, 2012 archive transfer) CPRE archive file 55/21/1a.

CPRE (Campaign to Protect Rural England) (2005) *Building on Barker* (written by N. Schoon), London: CPRE.

CPRE (2006) *Policy-based evidence making: The Policy Exchange's war against planning* (written by N. Schoon), London: CPRE.

CPRE (2009) '2026: a vision for the countryside'. Available at: www.cpre.org.uk/resources/cpre/about-cpre/item/download/517

CPRE (2010) *Green belts: A greener future*, London: CPRE and Natural England.

CPRE (2013) 'Policy guidance note on housing', March. Available at: www.cpre.org.uk/resources/policy-guidance-notes/item/download/2975

CPRE (2015) *Warm and green: Achieving affordable, low carbon energy while reducing impacts on the countryside*, London: CPRE.

CPRE (2016) 'Housing capacity on suitable brownfield land', October. Available at: https://www.cpre.org.uk/resources/housing-and-planning/housing/item/download/4733

CPRE (2017a) *Landlines: Why we need a strategic approach to land*, London: CPRE.

CPRE (2017b) 'Developers renege on affordable homes as countryside faces housing crisis', 6 June. Available at: https://www.cpre.org.uk/media-centre/latest-news-releases/item/4602-developers-renege-on-affordable-homes-as-countryside-faces-housing-crisis

CPRE (2017c) *Beauty betrayed: how reckless housing development threatens England's AONBs*, London: CPRE.

CPRE and Countryside Commission (2007a) 'Intrusion map: England, early 1960s'. Available at: www.cpre.org.uk/resources/countryside/tranquil-places/item/download/296

CPRE and Countryside Commission (2007b) 'Intrusion map: England, 2007'. Available at: www.cpre.org.uk/resources/countryside/tranquil-places/item/download/294

CPRE Sussex (no date) 'Making places'. Available at: https://www.ruralsussex.org.uk/making-places-report-released/

CPRE and Urbed (2015) *Shaping town and country*, London and Manchester: CPRE and Urbed, unpublished draft statement.

Crane, N. (2016) *The making of the British landscape*, London: Weidenfeld & Nicolson.

Crookston, M. (2014) *Garden suburbs of tomorrow? A new future for the cottage estates*, Abingdon: Routledge.

Crookston, M. (2016) 'Rethinking the "Town & Country" relationship', paper for the CPRE's Policy Committee and Board. Available at: www.cpre.org.uk/policy/policy-committee-meetings/item/download/4644

Daily Telegraph (2011) 'Conservatives given millions by property developers', 9 September. Available at: www.telegraph.co.uk/news/earth/hands-off-our-land/8754027/Conservatives-given-millions-by-property-developers.html

Daily Telegraph (2012) 'Hands off our land: housing estates will not be "plonked" next to villages, pledges David Cameron', 9 January. Available at: www.telegraph.co.uk/news/earth/hands-off-our-land/9002655/Hands-Off-Our-Land-Housing-estates-will-not-be-plonked-next-to-villages-pledges-David-Cameron.html

Davies, B. (2016) 'In filthy, dangerous accommodation, Britain's hidden homeless are suffering', *The Guardian*, 20 January.

DCLG (Department for Communities and Local Government) (2012) *National Planning Policy Framework*, London: DCLG.

DCLG (2016a) *Housing supply; net additional dwellings, England: 2015–16*, London: DCLG.

DCLG (2016b) *2014-based household projections: England, 2014–2039*, London: DCLG.

DCLG (2016c) 'New landmark with 200 communities now approving neighbourhood plans' press release, 11 July. Available at: https://www.gov.uk/government/news/new-landmark-with-200-communities-now-approving-neighbourhood-plans

DCLG (2017a) *Fixing our broken housing market* (Housing White Paper), London: DCLG.

DCLG (2017b) *English housing survey headline report, 2015–16*, London: DCLG.

Dixon, D. with Sinden, N. and Crabtree, T. (2017) *An independent review of housing in England's Areas of Outstanding Natural Beauty*, London: CPRE and the National Association of Areas of Outstanding Natural Beauty.

Donaldson, C. (2017a) *On the marshes*, Dorset: Little Toller.

Donaldson, C. (2017b) *A merry perambulation*, Medway: Swale Estuary Partnership.

Dorling, D. (2014) *All that is solid: The great housing disaster*, London: Allen Lane.

Eftec (Economics for the Environment Consultancy) (2010) 'Initial assessment of the costs and benefits of the National Forest', July. Available at: https://www.nationalforest.org/document/research/eftec_analysis.pdf

Ellis, H. and Henderson, K. (2014) *Rebuilding Britain: Planning for a better future*, Bristol: The Policy Press.

Evans, A.W. and Hartwich, O.M. (2005) *Unaffordable housing: Fables and myths*, London: Policy Exchange.

Evans, A.W. and Hartwich, O.M. (2006) *Better homes, greener cities*, London: Policy Exchange.

Farley, P. and Symmons Roberts, M. (2011) *Edgelands*, London: Jonathan Cape.

Flinders, M. (2012) *Defending politics: Why democracy matters in the twenty-first century*, Oxford: OUP.

Foot, M. (1975) *Aneurin Bevan 1945–1960*, London: Paladin Books.

Gardam, J. (2013) *Last friends*, London: Little Brown.

Greenberg, M. (2017) 'Tenants under siege: inside New York City's housing crisis', *New York Review of Books*, 17 August.

Griffith, M. and Jefferys, P. (2013) *Solutions for the housing shortage: How to build the 250,000 homes we need each year*, London: Shelter.

Hall, P. (2014) *Good cities, better lives: How Europe discovered the lost art of urbanism*, Abingdon: Routledge.

Hanley, L. (2007) *Estates: An intimate history*, London: Granta.

Hastings, M. (2006) 'Inaugural lecture', Museum of English Rural Life, 21 September.

Helm, D. (2015) 'In defence of the Green Belt'. Available at: www.dieterhelm.co.uk/assets/secure/documents/Green-Belt-Paper-.pdf

Holmans, A.E. (2005) *Historical statistics of housing in Britain*, Cambridge: Department of Land Economy.

Home Builders Federation (2017) *Reversing the decline of small housebuilders*, London: HBF.

Hoskins, W.G. (1979 [1955]) *The making of the English landscape*, London: Pelican.

House of Commons Library (2017) 'Tackling the under-supply of housing in England', June. Available at: http://researchbriefings.files.parliament.uk/documents/CBP-7671/CBP-7671.pdf

House of Lords Economic Affairs Select Committee (2016) *Building more homes*, London: House of Lords.

Jefferys, P. and Lloyd, T. (2017) *New civic housebuilding: Rediscovering our tradition of building beautiful and affordable homes*, London: Shelter.

Kent Messenger (2017) 'More, more, more: thousands of extra homes could be forced on borough', Maidstone edition, 21 September.

King, A. and Crewe, I. (2013) *The blunders of our governments*, London: Oneworld.

Kynaston, D. (2007) *Austerity Britain 1945–51*, London: Bloomsbury.

Lanchester, J. (2017) 'Between Victoria and Vauxhall', *London Review of Books*, 1 June, 39(11): 3–6.

Leunig, T. and Swaffield, J. (2008) *Cities unlimited: Making urban regeneration work*, London: Policy Exchange.

Lloyd, H. (ed) (2016) *Sustainable villages: Rural housing for the future*, London: Labour Coast and Country.

Lund, B. (2016) *Housing politics in the United Kingdom*, Bristol: The Policy Press.

Lyons, M. (2014) 'The Lyons housing review'. Available at: https://www.policyforum.labour.org.uk/uploads/editor/files/The_Lyons_Housing_Review_2.pdf

Matless, D. (1998) *Landscape and Englishness*, London: Reaktion Books.

McDonald, N. and Williams, P. (2014) *Planning for housing in England: Understanding recent changes in household formation rates and their implications for planning for housing in England*, London: RTPI.

McGhie, C. and Girling, R. (1996) *Local attraction: The design of new housing in the countryside*, London: CPRE.

McNamee, P., Benton, D., Brandmayr, C. and Elliott, J. (2017) 'Why the UK needs an ambitious clean growth plan now', Green Alliance. Available at: www.green-alliance.org.uk/UK_needs_clean_growth_plan_now.php

Meek, J. (2014) 'Where will we live?', *London Review of Books*, 9 January, 36/1.

Millar, P. (2013) 'A village ruined by the PM's "plonkers"', *Sunday Times*, 29 September. Available at: https://www.thetimes.co.uk/article/a-village-ruined-by-the-pms-plonkers-p6h5vd0gh5q

Minton, A. (2017) *Big capital? Who is London for?*, London: Penguin.

Moore, R. (2017) 'North West Cambridge: a model for affordable urban housing?', *The Observer*, 10 September. Available at: https://www.theguardian.com/environment/2017/sep/10/building-trust-into-greener-housing-north-west-cambridge-development

Morphet, J. and Clifford, B. (2017) 'Local authority direct provision of housing', National Planning Forum and RTPI, December 2017. Available at: http://rtpi.org.uk/media/2619006/Local-authority-direct-provision-of-housing.pdf

Morton, A. (2011) *Cities for growth: Solutions to our planning problems*, London: Policy Exchange.

Murie, A. (2016) *The right to buy? Selling off public and social housing*, Bristol: The Policy Press.

National Housing Federation (2017a) 'Demise of the Nimby: changing attitudes to building new homes', February, London: National Housing Federation. Available at: www.housing.org.uk/resource-library/browse/demise-of-the-nimby-changing-attitudes-to-building-new-homes/

National Housing Federation (2017b) 'How many homes did housing associations build in 2016/17?', May. Available at: www.housing.org.uk/resource-library/browse/how-many-homes-did-housing-associations-build-in-2016-17/

Newsome, S., Carpenter, E. and Kendall, P. (2015) *The Hoo Peninsula landscape*, Swindon: Historic England. ONS (Office for National Statistics) (2014) 'Households and household composition: 2001–11'. Available at: www.ons.gov.uk/peoplepopulationandcommunity/birthsdeathsandmarriages/families/articles/householdsandhousehold composition inenglandandwales/2014-05-29/pdf

O'Shaughnessy, J. (2013) 'Winning over aspiring voters in 2015', in R. Shorthouse and B. Stagg (eds) *Tory modernisation 2.0: The future of the Conservative Party*, London: Bright Blue.

Papworth, T. (2015) *The green noose*, London: ASI.

Pavord, A. (2016) *Landskipping*, London: Bloomsbury.

Policy Exchange (2017) 'Farming tomorrow: British agriculture after Brexit', August. Available at: https://policyexchange.org.uk/wp-content/uploads/2017/07/Farming_Tomorrow.pdf

Pryor, F. (2010) *The making of the British landscape*, London: Allen Lane.

Raynsford, N. (2016) *Substance not spin*, Bristol: The Policy Press.

Resolution Foundation (2017) '21st century Britain has seen a 30 per cent increase in second home ownership', 19 August. Available at: www.resolutionfoundation.org/media/press-releases/21st-century-britain-has-seen-a-30-per-cent-increase-in-second-home-ownership/

Reynolds, F. (2016) *The fight for beauty*, London: Oneworld.

Rowley, T. (2006) *The English landscape in the twentieth century*, London: Hambledon Continuum.

Ryan-Collins, J., Lloyd, T. and Macfarlane, L. (2017) *Rethinking the economics of land and housing*, London: Zed Books.

Samuel, R. (1994) *Theatres of memory*, London: Verso.

Scruton, R. (2012) *Green philosophy: How to think seriously about the planet*, London: Atlantic.

Shelter (2017a) *Unsettled and insecure: The toll insecure private renting is taking on English families*, London: Shelter.

Shelter (2017b) 'Phantom homes: planning permissions, completions and profits', Research Briefing, July. Available at: https://england.shelter.org.uk/__data/assets/pdf_file/0005/1396778/2017_07_07_Phantom_Homes_-_Profits,_Planning_Permissions_and_Completions.pdf

Shoard, M. (2002) 'Edgelands', in J. Jenkins (ed) *Remaking the landscape: The changing face of Britain*, London: Profile, pp 117–46.

Short, B. (2006) *England's landscape: The South East*, London: Collins.

Sinnett, D., Carmichael, L., Williams, K. and Miner, P. (2014) *From wasted space to living spaces*, London: CPRE and the University of the West of England.

Sloman, L., Hopkinson, L. and Taylor, I. (2017) *The impact of road projects in England*, London: CPRE.

Smart Cities Dive (no date) 'Wenzhou, China builds Asia's largest underground sewage treatment plant'. Available at: www.smartcitiesdive.com/ex/sustainablecitiescollective/wenzhou-china-builds-asia-s-largest-underground-sewage-treatment-plan/1204751/

Spiers, S. (2016) 'Visiting Alconbury Weald, Huntingdon', Blog, 9 September. Available at: https://cpreviewpoint.wordpress.com/2016/09/09/visiting-alconbury-weald-huntingdon/

Swinford, G. (1987) *Jubilee boy*, Filkins: The Filkins Press.

Tapper, J. (2017) 'Countryside faces "fuel poverty" crisis', *Observer*, 20 August. Available at: https://www.theguardian.com/uk-news/2017/aug/19/rural-areas-suffer-worst-fuel-poverty-insulation-energy-prices

The Observer (2010) 'Tory MP calls for local government planning to be replaced by "chaos"', 19 December. Available at: https://www.theguardian.com/politics/2010/dec/18/coalition-local-planning-boles-chaos

This is Money (2015) 'Top ten holiday home hotspots revealed: Cornwall is favourite – and 165,000 Britons own a second property for leisure', 24 April. Available at: www.thisismoney.co.uk/money/buytolet/article-3052013/Top-ten-holiday-home-hotspots-revealed-Cornwall-top.html

Thompson, C. (2017) 'Fruits of the money tree', *New Statesman*, 6–12 October.

Transparency International (2017) *Faulty Towers: Understanding the impact of overseas corruption on the London property market*, London: Transparency International.

Urban, F. (2015) 'Germany, country of tenants', *Built Environment*, 41(2): 183–95.

Urbed (2014) 'Uxcester Garden City'. Available at: http://urbed. coop/wolfson-economic-prize

Urbed (2015) 'Sheffield Garden City? Options for long-term urban growth'. Available at: http://urbed.coop/projects/sheffield-garden-city-options-long-term-urban-growth

Waine, P. and Hilliam, O. (2016) *22 ideas that saved the English countryside*, London: Frances Lincoln.

Walker, T. (2016) *On solid ground: Encouraging landowners to invest in rural affordable housing*, London: CPRE.

Walker, T. (2017) *Needless demand: How a focus on need can help solve the housing crisis*, London: CPRE.

Wassenberg, F. (2015) 'Meeting the British housing challenge: Dutch experience and reflections', *Built Environment*, 41(2): 211–26.

Williams, J. (2017) 'Who is really benefiting from the Manchester city centre housing boom?', *Manchester Evening News*, 9 October.

Williams, R. (1993 [1973]) *The country and the city*, London: Hogarth.

Williams-Ellis, C. (1996 [1928]) *England and the octopus*, London: CPRE.

Index

References to figures are in *italics*